WORKING MEN'S COLLEGE

LIBRARY REGULATIONS

If I Forget Thee

IF 1 FORGET THEE

H & N BEN TWICH

If I forget thee, O Jerusalem, let my right hand forget her cunning.

If I do not remember thee, let my tongue cleave to the roof of my mouth; if I prefer not Jerusalem above my chief joy.

from Psalm 137

IF I FORGET THEE

some chapters of autobiography
1912–1920

HELEN BENTWICH

Elek London

© 1973 The Friends of the Hebrew University of Jerusalem

Published in Great Britain by
Paul Elek Books Limited
54–8 Caledonian Road London N1 9RN

ISBN 0 236 15450 8

*Produced by computer-controlled phototypesetting,
using OCR input techniques, and printed offset by
UNWIN BROTHERS LIMITED
The Gresham Press, Old Woking, Surrey*

Contents

Publisher's Note   ix

I Introduce Myself   1

1910, 1912, 1914   Travel   12

1914–1915   England   30

1915–1916   Cairo   43

1916–1917   Woolwich Arsenal   75

1917–1918   The Land Army (1)   107

1918–1919   The Land Army (2)   140

1919–1920   Jerusalem   156

Illustrations

Bookplate designed by a cousin for Helen and Norman Bentwich in 1920 (*frontispiece*)

Helen Bentwich as a child at Chartridge with her father and Ellis (*facing page 38*)

Helen Bentwich's mother (*facing page 39*)

The guard of honour after the Bentwich wedding, September 1915 (*facing page 54*)

1st Whitechapel Girl Guides leaving camp at Chartridge, August 1915 (*facing page 55*)

Reggie and the other test room men from Woolwich Arsenal, 1916 (*facing page 55*)

The Levis motorcycle near Tring, July 1917 (*facing page 150*)

Talking to the Queen, Buckingham Palace, March 1918 (*facing page 150*)

Helen and Norman Bentwich in Jerusalem (*facing page 151*)

Norman on his way to the synagogue in the Old City (*facing page 151*)

Sir Herbert Samuel with Lord Balfour and General Allenby in Jerusalem (*facing page 166*)

Sir Herbert Samuel as High Commissioner (*facing page 167*)

Statement signed by General Sir Louis Bols, Chief Administrator of Palestine, and given to Sir Herbert Samuel (*page 170*)

Publisher's Note

Helen Bentwich died suddenly in April 1972 after a long and active life. So active that at the age of eighty she was planning the next volume of her autobiography, though this one was not quite finished. It was to deal with the years after she and Norman Bentwich had come back to England, and thus the central core of her life: her devoted service to the London County Council for over thirty years and to the Socialist cause generally. Her main concern was always education, especially for those who had missed out on it in childhood. Hence her passionate belief in the evening institute system and her influential lectures to the troops in Germany directly before the Labour victory of 1945.

This volume of public struggles and triumphs will now never be written and we are left with this fragment covering the years up to 1920. It is probably much more fascinating than any fuller account could have been. For it shows how parental influences shaped Helen Bentwich and turned her into the young woman she became, Jewish by faith, English by temperament, idealistic, independent, full of practical good sense. It also shows an outstanding individual reacting to a particularly violent period of history, the First World War. In some ways she was more fortunate than many others at the time, for she had connections in high places and could make choices, instead of having things decided for her. But the fact remains that she chose to lay aside the tennis parties and polite 'economy campaigns' of her class and instead shared the life of ordinary working women in wartime—travelling to work in the dark for a twelve-hour shift at the Woolwich Arsenal, pulling up weeds or spreading muck in the fields of Hertfordshire, wearing the clothes appropriate to the job and the weather. She also chose to give up all idea of returning to her husband in Cairo before the war was over.

The budding Socialist kept in touch with the versatile Zionist during the three and a half years of their separation by an almost daily flow of letters. Helen's side of the correspondence is well represented in the chapters of this book, as are some of her letters to her mother when she was reunited with Norman Bentwich in Palestine after the war. They describe with an authenticity which would be missing from reminiscence exactly what it felt like to live at the time and how different were the realities of existence compared with the slogans bruited abroad by officials.

At the beginning of the war we find her complaining that she had never 'done anything worthwhile, except get married'. At the end we find that our breath has been taken away by the sheer range of experience she buckled under her belt. And even when she returned to being a wife and hostess again in Jerusalem it was only a matter of days before she was organizing work for unemployed Jewish girls and trying to get to know the Moslem women.

The large red house in Hampstead where Helen Bentwich had lived with her husband until his death only the year before her own was redolent with memories of their life together. The walls were lined with books, many of which had been written by Norman Bentwich, uniquely qualified as he was to write about Arab-Jewish relations and the building of the state of Israel. Jerusalem lay always in their thoughts and was invoked in their bookplates. But Helen's own life, which was mainly conducted in England without any apparent compromise or disloyalty to her husband, was oddly unrepresented. She clearly felt this omission and was specially pleased to have this volume accepted for publication in her eightieth year. It is indeed a valuable social document in its own right, as well as showing the liveliness, honesty and acuteness of observation which the best autobiographies possess.

I Introduce Myself

I was born at 29 Pembridge Gardens, Notting Hill Gate, London, in 1892, the fifth child of a family of six. My parents were both Jewish, my father belonging to the third generation of his family to be born in England, my mother to the first. My brother Jack was the eldest of our family, born in 1884: my only sister, Alice, was born the next year, my brother Cecil in 1887, Hugh in 1889, and my youngest brother, Ellis, in 1894.

We lived in Pembridge Gardens until 1910, and were a happy, united family, though often difficult individually. We found my father, with his strict religious orthodoxy and his narrow Victorian views, especially about the upbringing of his daughters, rather a trial, but he was a kindly and generous man, and did his best to understand us. He was one of the leaders of Anglo-Jewry, active in social work for the Jewish community, both for their material welfare and their religious education, and a pillar of the New West End Synagogue. He was also active in the wider community, being particularly interested in working-class housing. In 1899 he had bought a small house at Chartridge, a hamlet on a spur of the Chilterns, in Buckinghamshire, which by 1914 had been expanded into quite an imposing residence with a very large garden, a small farm, many fields and a few woods. He was later a Justice of the Peace for Buckinghamshire, and sat in court at the small town of Chesham, three miles from Chartridge. He was interested in politics, being a Liberal Unionist. He was the senior partner in a banking firm, A. Keyser & Co.

My mother was a lovable, gifted and very unusual person.

1

Though not brought up in the orthodox traditions of my father, she nevertheless loyally supported him in the running of her home. She had married when just nineteen—my father was seven years older—and had been educated at Bedford College in the days when chaperons had to be provided for the students while lectured by men. She, too, played her part in the Jewish community, but her main interest was in education. She was a manager of schools in the East End, under the London School Board, and some of my earliest recollections are of the parties she gave at Pembridge Gardens for the teachers in these schools. Later, the older pupils from these schools, with their teachers, were invited to 'hay-making' parties at Chartridge. In 1902, when the responsibility for education was transferred from the School Boards to the local councils, she was co-opted one of the two women members of the Buckinghamshire Education Committee, remaining a member till her death in 1935. Although Father was so reactionary in his views regarding his daughters, he was extremely proud of his wife. Alice and I said he recognized three sexes: men, women and mother. But, for all her activities, she was a wonderful mother, never letting her public work stand in the way of the welfare of her children. We were never the kind of children who saw our mother for a few odd hours in the evening. We went everywhere with her, before we went to school, and I attended many functions at the schools in the East End before I was of school age myself. We went out in the carriage with her nearly every day; and when Chartridge became an important part of our lives, she would take us for long walks, teaching us the names of the wild flowers, and where to find them. She even encouraged us to 'help' her in the garden, which she loved so much.

We were of the generation lucky in having family nurses. Ours, Emma Pitt—Nana, as we called her—remained with the family for over fifty years. An observing Christian, she never missed attending church on Sunday, refused to sew on that day, and disliked it if she was expected to take us by train on her Sabbath. Nevertheless, she was watchful to see that we never broke any of the rules of *our* Sabbath, and 'heard' us say our Hebrew prayers every night. (Father, in his dressing-gown, took us for prayers every morning, until one by one we rebelled. My particular rebellion occurred when I heard my brothers thanking

God they had not been born women!) Nana came from Glouces-
ter, and it was from her that I first realized what it was to be born
privileged, and learnt about class distinctions. When I found our
old clothes and toys were being sent to her young nephews and
nieces, I objected, and insisted that Mother buy them new ones. I
think the seeds of my socialism were planted by her, though she
would have been shocked had she known this, for she came from
a good Liberal family. We all loved her dearly, and were deeply
grieved when she died in 1935, the same year as mother.

From an early age we discussed politics freely at home.
Mother was a Liberal, and Father's brother-in-law, Herbert
Samuel, was a Liberal Member of Parliament. Alice was a
Socialist, and was the Honorary Secretary of a group of young
intellectuals, who called themselves the 'Utopians'. They were
influenced by H. G. Wells, who was their President. Meetings
were often held in our house, and I, an untidy schoolgirl, would
creep in at the back, unnoticed, when I should have been doing
my homework. By the time I was fourteen, I declared myself a
Socialist too. I also decided I was an atheist, because I found my
father's particular form of orthodox Judaism distasteful, especially in its attitude towards my sex. I resented having to attend
Synagogue whenever we were in London on Saturdays or the
Holy Days, and having to sit in the gallery, segregated from my
brothers and all other males. When we were in the country,
Father gave the service, which we were all forced to attend.
Hugh, also, was a Socialist; the other three boys were less
interested in politics, but enjoyed arguing against us.

We moved from Pembridge Gardens to my grandfather's
house in Porchester Terrace after his death in 1909. The house
was enlarged and modernized before we moved in, and both
there, and when we stayed in the enlarged house at Chartridge,
we had eight servants. As I grew older, I became ashamed of
taking my friends home to what I considered such unnecessary
opulence, although I must confess I always enjoyed the comfort
in which I lived. And my friends were pleased to come and play
tennis on our excellent court in the garden. By then, the family
were beginning to go their own ways. Jack, though he lived at
home during the week, would be out every night, and away on
his yacht each week-end. Political arguments became more
acrimonious, and many times Hugh and I would be sent from the

table at meal-times, because we had been unduly rude . Here we realized the advantages of still having a devoted Nana, for we would finish our meals in her room upstairs. Later, both Jack and Hugh married non-Jews, and my father never saw Hugh again. Jack was a partner in the banking firm, and though he saw him daily, he had as little as possible to do with him, and never met his wife. He cut them both out of his will. I believe this situation made him extremely unhappy, but he was forced by his inner convictions to live up to his principles. Mother, though always striving to be loyal to her husband, would see them occasionally, without his knowledge. But I know the estrangement was a great and unnecessary grief to her.

I was a troublesome child, mainly, I believe, because from early years I resented the differences made between me and my brothers, and the lack of the freedom which was allowed to them. I never went out alone till I was nearly grown-up, and although I enjoyed going about with Nana, later, when I was 'taken out' by a French or German governess (they came to us on alternate days), I would rebel, run away, and cause trouble. Whenever I was scolded for disobedience or bad behaviour, my invariable answer was: 'I'd be all right if I were a boy.' In my day-dreams I was always a boy, and my favourite dream at one time was that I'd only just been born, and someone said: 'A mistake has been made. It's a boy, not a girl.' I learnt the facts of life early on from my brothers, but Mother never talked to me of such things, which was, I think, the usual attitude towards sex at that time, though unthinkable today for anyone as intelligent and forward-looking as she was. I was so troublesome that I was rapidly becoming what is today called 'maladjusted'. Mother took me to see a woman called Mrs Archer; I believe her to have been the wife of the man who translated Ibsen. She was, I imagine, some kind of child psychologist. I sat in a rather dark room with her and my mother, while she asked me questions. I still have a horror of what I call 'probing'; and I refused to answer. The questions went on and on. So I used the only weapon possible to a small girl imprisoned, as I thought I was, with two grown-up women determined to make me answer. Even Mother seemed somehow to have become a stranger. I screamed, and never stopped screaming till I found myself with Mother in the carriage going home. I was in deep disgrace, and Mother said she was ashamed

4

of me. But I was not taken there again. We were never actually punished, beyond being deprived of 'treats'. This time, I felt no shame: I still think I was right.

My brothers taught me to read by the time I was three, and from then onwards I read everything I could find. They also taught Ellis and me to play chess. When I was five and he only three, we would play for hours, sitting under the nursery table. He was a much better player than I was. Unfortunately, our family doctor, a very old-fashioned person, found us playing one day, and told mother to stop us, or we would get 'brain fever', which frightened me, as this was the mysterious illness which killed off the good children in many of the old-fashioned books I read. From my fourth to my seventh year I went to a kindergarten class, held in the house of some of my cousins, the Waleys. I enjoyed the games, and being with the other children, but found the rest uninteresting. At seven I went to Norland Place School, a private school in very unsuitable buildings in Holland Park Avenue. It still exists there. The teaching was excellent and enlightened. We learnt history as something progressive and exciting, not just as a succession of kings and wars, and we were encouraged to talk of the problems of the day, at a time when 'current affairs' as a subject was unknown. In my last year there, when I was fourteen, we were told to write a list of what we considered the ten most urgent reforms needed. I still have the list I wrote. I advocated the abolition of the Aliens Act, that horse-racing, betting and gambling should be forbidden, that all Public Schools should have County Council scholars, the abolition of the game laws, that there should be old age pensions, that there should be only one public house for every three hundred inhabitants, that anyone sweating labour should be prosecuted and the fining of workers should be abolished, that no religion should be taught in council schools, that no more than three sleep in one room, and that the rents of small houses and cottages should be reduced. I am envious of one of my friends who wrote there should be a green belt all round London, where no building was to be allowed. Curiously, none of us advocated women's suffrage.

I made friends easily at school, and was good at games and the subjects I liked, which were history, literature and arithmetic. But I never troubled to work at any subject in which I was not interested. I was put into a class of girls older than myself which it was thought might spur me on. But it failed, and my reports were worse each term. I was the ringleader in all school mischief and disobedience, and when I left in 1906 Miss Langhorn, the headmistress, singled me out before the whole school as a girl from whom much had been expected, but who had disappointed everyone. She added that she was glad I was leaving. I was not ashamed, only furiously angry.

I believe my mother had to do a good deal of persuading before my father would consent to my going to St Paul's Girls' School, which had then been open for two years. To his way of thinking, it was much too 'modern'. I did so badly in the entrance examination that I was placed in a very low form. This shocked me. I had friends at the school who were two forms higher, and I wanted to be with them. So my first day at the school, I walked boldly into the room of Miss Gray, the High Mistress. She was a charming Irish woman, with a keen sense of humour. Some found her alarming, but in those days I had not learnt to be frightened of people. When she asked me, with, I imagine, some amusement, what I wanted, I explained that I wanted to be in the same form as my friends. She thought for a while, then told me she had had a very bad report about me from Norland Place, but that, if I really meant to turn over a new leaf, and gave no trouble, she would let me move into the form where I wanted to be. For the first time I felt ashamed of my past, and promised her I really would work hard and behave well. She sent me away, saying: 'But of course, if you cause any trouble, and don't work hard, down you go to where you are now.' I never was demoted, and worked fairly hard though still neglected the language lessons which I so disliked. We worked in 'sets', moving up for the subjects in which we were good, and down for those in which we were bad. English literature was my favourite subject, and I was soon in a high 'set' for that, and later for chemistry as well.

I was not distinguished academically at school, and failed to reach the highest form—the eighth. I have since been grieved that I was so unmusical that Gustav Holst, our music master, turned me out of the singing class. I was allowed to read whatever I liked in the library instead. I was, however, very good at both hockey and cricket, and, when I was older, helped to coach the other girls. But I was not able to play in the school teams. From the opening of the school there had been a number of Jewish girls, and, as the matches were on Saturdays, it was understood that the Jewish girls were not in the teams. I think that is the only real disadvantage I have felt in being Jewish in all my life. Special kosher dinners were provided for the Jewish girls, but we sat at ordinary tables with our friends, and the fact that we had different food was unnoticed. I grew up proud of being Jewish, however much I resented the narrow religious observances imposed on me by my father.

As both my parents came from large families, I had a great number of relatives, including thirty-five first cousins, and innumerable cousins of the second degree. Some were at St Paul's with me, and were my greatest friends, especially Evelyn and Ruth Waley. And Olive Franklin, although not at the same school, completed a very happy and congenial quartette. Perhaps it was because of my numerous relations, most of whom lived within walking distance of each other, that I made fewer lasting friendships at school than I might otherwise have done. We were, probably, too 'clannish'. Every Friday night, when we were in London, my aunts and uncles would gather at our house, or at my grandfather's while he was alive, and our house at Chartridge was always full of 'family'. When we lived in Porchester Terrace, Herbert Samuel lived two doors away, and I saw much of him and his wife and children.

After leaving school in 1910 I spent three years at Bedford College. Although I had failed to matriculate, I was allowed to attend lectures at the College, in the way my mother had done many years before. At first, I studied botany and zoology, mainly in the old buildings in Baker Street, reputed to be the home of the imaginary Sherlock Holmes. My ambition then was to be a farmer, but my parents wisely said I must wait till I was twenty-five. If, by then, I still felt the same, they promised they would set me up with a farm. (When I was twenty-five I was married, and working in the Land Army during the First World War, but I had lost all desire to make farming a career.)

As soon as I left school, my sister Alice, who was then a devoted Care Committee worker in London's East End, persuaded me to form a company of Girl Guides in the LCC school at Commercial Street, next door to Toynbee Hall, which was her particular concern. She felt that the older girls at the school

7

needed some healthy activity and interest to occupy them after school hours, and during the holidays. I knew nothing of the movement, but was immediately interested, and became an extremely enthusiastic Guide Captain. Miss Agnes Baden-Powell, the sister of the Chief Scout was, in those early days of the movement, its President. There were then few rules and little red tape, and each captain was able to experiment and to develop along her own lines. Almost all the girls were Jewish, many from immigrant homes where only Yiddish was spoken. The rest were the daughters of street-vendors. I soon became extremely interested in the lives of the East End girls; their backgrounds, their opportunities, and their general outlook on life made for me a fascinating study. They only needed me for two evenings a week, occasionally on Sundays for expeditions to the country, and for a fortnight in the summer-holidays for a camp.

While I was still at school, I was enlisted to go on one evening a week to teach English to foreign girls at the West Central Jewish Girls' Club, in Dean Street, Soho. There was a strong tradition in the Anglo-Jewish community that members of the wealthier families should devote some of their time to helping those who were less fortunate, and my parents encouraged their children to pursue these voluntary activities. But my father had rigid Victorian views about his daughters earning their own living. Alice was such a skilled Care Committee worker that when the London County Council took over the organization they would have employed her in an official capacity. But my father was adamant in refusing to allow this.

The West Central Jewish Girls' Club, where I taught English in a very amateur fashion, had been founded by Lily Montagu, a deeply religious woman and a dedicated social worker, when she was barely out of the schoolroom. She had been helped by my father's sister, Beatrice, later the wife of Herbert Samuel. Lily was one of the founders of Liberal Judaism, and frequently conducted services and preached sermons in their synagogues.

These unimportant efforts of mine in social work drew me away from any idea of farming, and I decided to undergo some training. I enrolled at Bedford College, as a student in the four-term course in social hygiene, and at the end of the course passed an examination (the only one I ever passed in my whole life) and emerged with a certificate. This led to my working, in the day-time as well as in the evenings, at the West Central Club, which had by then moved to Alfred Place, the other side of Oxford Street, into a new building with a hostel attached, and an employment bureau. These buildings were destroyed by a bomb during the Second World War, with tragic loss of life. For a few years after this, I was the President of the Club.

I was interested in working for the club, and especially in visiting the homes of the girls, and their places of work. But I never enjoyed my work there in the same way as I did the hours I spent with the Guides. I was not personally responsible for any section of the Club, and never able to carry out my own theories, or initiate experiments. But I made friends with many of the Club members, especially with those of my own age, and was captivated by what seemed to me, at that time, the mysterious charms of Soho. The area on the north side of Oxford Street I found sordid and uninteresting. It was here I made my first acquaintance with prostitutes. Deeply shocked, I wrote about them to the police, only to receive a kindly reply explaining the law. I would talk about them with my men friends, and those I danced with at parties, because I felt that here was a problem which must be tackled from the angle of the men who used them. It seemed to me simple: so long as men used prostitutes, there would always be girls ready to be used. Somehow, men must be persuaded *not* to use them. Later, I got to know some of these girls. Often the alternative to prostitution was a youth spent working in overcrowded, overheated tailors' workshops for miserable wages, making clothes for rich men and women. I think many of them, when starting on the career of prostitution, hoped to find a rich patron to 'keep' them in luxury. A few did; some married; but too many died of disease. I developed an enormous respect for the girls at the Club who, despite the squalor of the lives they led, and despite the temptations of the 'West End', kept 'straight', and became valued members of society. Such was the attitude towards actresses at that time, that any girl making the stage a career was no longer allowed to be a member of the Club.

When war was declared, on 4 August, 1914, I was in charge of my Girl Guide camp at Chartridge. I was then twenty-two years old, and, by present-day standards, very young for my age. Although a Socialist, I was never a pacifist; as soon as possible I

9

joined a small VAD detachment, which was started in Chesham. Alice extended her work in the East End, to help in the workshops set up for unemployed women and girls. Jack, who had always been keen on the sea, soon joined the Navy. Ellis, who should have gone to Oxford in the autumn, joined an Officers' Training Unit, and was later commissioned in 'Kitchener's Army'. We were a lucky family, as they both survived the war. Cecil, who had very poor sight, was unable to join the forces. In 1914 he was a partner in the publishing firm of Routledge, but he worked for some time helping to receive and establish the large numbers of Belgian refugees who arrived in England. Later, he and my father both joined the 'National Guard', a voluntary organization of civilians, who, among other things, met the soldiers at Victoria, as they arrived back from the front, helped those on leave to find their way to their homes or to billets, and did all that amateurs could do for the wounded. My mother worked some nights a week at the canteen for soldiers at Victoria station.

Hugh was abroad, in Brussels, when war broke out. While at Cambridge he had been drawn into the suffrage movement, and became an active member of the Men's Social and Political Union, which supported the militant suffragettes. He left Cambridge in 1910, and soon afterwards attacked Winston Churchill, an ardent opponent of Women's Suffrage, in the corridor of a railway train, attempting to strike him with a dog-whip. (Hugh said he actually hit him, but Churchill denied this.) He was arrested and tried, and committed to prison for six weeks. My mother was in the court, where Churchill appeared as a witness. In 1921, when she was in Jerusalem staying with her brother-in-law, Herbert Samuel, then the High Commissioner in Palestine, Churchill, who was at that time Colonial Secretary, came to stay. Mother was greatly perturbed lest he should recognize her—fortunately, he did not.

Soon after Hugh was released from prison, he set fire to a railway train. Curiously, he chose the line on which we travelled to Chesham station, and was recognized. For many weeks, he escaped arrest, hiding, I have always believed, above Henderson's book shop—known as the 'Bombshop'—in Charing Cross Road, now Collett's book shop. During that period, our home in Porchester Terrace was continually under the surveillance of

10

detectives. Eventually he was caught, and sentenced to nine months' imprisonment. He was one of the first to go on hunger-strike, and to be forcibly fed. This lasted for some weeks, and was seriously undermining his health. As by then there were a number of women also on hunger-strike, the Government brought in a Bill, known as the 'Cat and Mouse Act', which allowed for the release of those whose health was being affected by the forcible feeding. After they had recovered, they were to be arrested again, and sent back to prison. Hugh came home to recover, but soon made his escape to the Continent, dressed as a woman, together with others who had been released. One of them was Elsie Duval, whom he eventually married. They went first to Dresden, and later to Brussels. Once again, after his escape, we were closely watched by detectives, and they would sometimes follow Alice and me as we set out in the morning, believing, I imagine, that we were unaware of their presence. But this stopped after Alice, one day, turned round to the detective and said: 'If you insist on following me, you might at least carry my dispatch case.' This the abashed young man did—but we were followed no more. As two detectives were always outside the house two doors away, guarding Herbert Samuel, who was then the Home Secretary, the maids in the two houses had an enjoyable time.

Hugh and the other 'suffragettes' would have been immediately arrested and re-imprisoned, had they returned to England. On the outbreak of war, an amnesty was declared, and they were allowed to come home. Hugh was found unfit to join the forces—due to the forcible feeding—but obtained work on the staff of Woolwich Arsenal.

1910, 1912, 1914

Travel

My parents were enthusiastic travellers and, for people living the conventional life which they lived in England, unusually adventurous. This, of course, was long before the days of package tours. They enlisted the help of Messrs Thomas Cook in arranging time-tables, and booking rooms in hotels, when they had decided exactly where they wanted to go, and what they wanted to see. It was also before the days when passports were necessary, though my cautious father always had one with him. The only time I remember it being used was when we wanted to see the view from some military observation post. So unused were the officials to seeing a British passport, that they made out the permit in the name of Sir Edward Grey, who was the Foreign Minister who had signed the passport.

My father would never let us relax our Jewish orthodox traditions during our travels, and elaborate arrangements had to be made never to travel on the Sabbath, although it was accepted that travelling on the sea was permissible if the journey neither began nor ended on a Saturday. It was understood that we would be living without meat on our travels, unless we were in a town where a kosher restaurant was available. The hotels we stayed in were often very primitive, and at times verminous: bathrooms were generally non-existent, and the only means of travel, other than train or ship, was by horse-drawn carriages, for neither of my parents could ride. I enjoyed this form of unsophisticated travel. We managed to keep well—and clean—and saw far more of the countries we visited, and the inhabitants, than many do who travel today.

The first time I accompanied them on one of these interesting journeys was in 1910, during my last year at school. Miss Gray, enlightened and broad-minded in this as in so many other ways, agreed to my missing part of the Easter term, saying it would benefit my general education. Alice was with us, too, and we went to Dalmatia, Bosnia, Herzegovina and Croatia, all then part of the Austro-Hungarian Empire, and to the independent state of Montenegro. At that time many of the town-dwellers, as well as the peasants, still wore their picturesque native costumes. We were particularly enthralled by Cettigne, the capital of Montenegro, which we reached after a long drive from Cattaro, on the coast. The drive was made more interesting, for me (though not for my mother) by the fact that the driver of the carriage in which we were travelling, with Father and Alice following in another carriage, was quite drunk, and while he was driving at a furious pace we had to jump out, to avoid being hurtled over a precipice. We waited, in a thick mist, till the other carriage arrived, Mother afraid of being attacked by brigands, while I was longing for some such adventure to befall us. In Cettigne, a small primitive town, where the palace was called the 'Billiardo', as it boasted a billiard-table, we saw the king and his sons strolling along the street every evening. We visited the town school—Mother liked to visit schools in every country—which had three hundred boys and a hundred girls in a very primitive building, and were told that education was free and compulsory.

Two years later, we went to the same countries again, staying in different places, and visiting some of the lovely little islands in the Adriatic, then quite unspoilt. Once our ship broke down, and we were landed on the island of Cunzola, which, in 1815, had belonged to the British. On the ship was a local politician, who spoke good English. He and Father had a long talk, mainly about Ireland, because the politician belonged to a party which was striving to set up a united Serbia and break away from the Austro-Hungarian Empire, and he was anxious to know what steps Ireland was taking to break away from Britain. Father told him that his brother-in-law was a Cabinet Minister in the Liberal government, and our friend said he would like to write to him. At Cunzola, he took us to a club, which was full of others who were, like him, plotting for a united Serbia. After the outbreak of the war, he wrote a few times to Herbert Samuel, who said the information he received was valuable. When the war was over, he was a delegate to the Paris Peace Conference, and later came to England, and stayed with us at Chartridge. We never heard from him after that, but were told he had 'died suddenly' in some riots.

Having been to Sarajevo, then a lovely town with oriental bazaars, we could later understand the political significance of the assassination of the Austrian Archduke there in 1914—but not its ghastly global repercussions.

In the spring of 1914 we went to Egypt, then under the protection of Britain, and on to Palestine, Syria and the Lebanon, all part of the Turkish Empire, and finally to Constantinople. We sailed from Marseilles on the P & O liner *Morea*, arriving at Port Said early on 1 April. Being an ardent Kipling enthusiast, I was looking forward to my first glimpse of the East in what I then believed was one of the wicked and immoral towns of the world. I found it incredibly dirty, with heaps of filth at every corner, flies swarming over the food in the shops and around the running, diseased eyes of the children, mangy goats, starving cats and featherless bleeding chickens roaming the streets. If this were vice, I thought, give me virtue.

We took the train, later in the day, to Cairo, where we stayed at the Savoy Hotel. My parents scorned Shepheards, believing it to be showy and vulgar. The Savoy was more select—and extremely comfortable. We conscientiously 'did' all the tourist sights: innumerable mosques, the museums, the bazaars, the Pyramids; we rode on camels out to Sakhara, which I felt was quite adventurous of my parents. I disliked Cairo, hating the dirt, the poverty and the general messiness. I fear that I was looking on it with the eyes of a London social worker. But I have never fallen victim to 'the magic of the East', though I have always loved the sunshine, and the brilliant flowering trees and shrubs. It was cool during our days in Cairo—and it actually rained.

We knew only one person in Cairo, and he came to see us, and accompanied us on some of our sightseeing. He was Norman Bentwich, then a lecturer in the Law School, who had once spent a week-end with us at Chartridge, when we had had long walks and talks together. Although he was nine years my senior, and

14

extremely learned, he listened kindly to my half-baked views on politics and life in general. We had tea with him in the flat he shared with a delightful Scotsman, James Baxter.

We left Cairo on 5 April, and I wrote in my diary: 'I am very sorry to leave here.' I realize, after all these years, it was Norman I was sorry to be leaving, and not Cairo.

I continue with extracts from the diary I kept at the time.

5 April We went back to Port Said by train, and then got into little boats, which took us out to the SS *Tewkkiah*, of the Khedivial Mail Line. It was packed with people of all nationalities: the third-class passengers mainly sat in the hold, and were quiet and orderly. The second-and first-class passengers were not so orderly. They were German and American, Armenian and Circassian, Greek, French, Italian and a few English. There were some young English girls and boys who formed part of a troupe going to perform in Beirut. Fortunately, it was a calm night. I shared my cabin with a German woman, and a Jewess from Whitechapel. My parents shared theirs with large cockroaches, and spent most of the night sleeping on couches in the saloon. The captain was English.

6 April We arrived at Jaffa at 6 am, and David Yellin, the head of the Jewish community in Jerusalem, came on board to meet us. We had to jump from the gangway into small boats, amid a tremendous hubbub and confusion. When it is rough, passengers cannot land at Jaffa, because the small boats cannot then manoeuvre the passage through a line of dangerous rocks. We had literally to fight our way through the customs. After breakfast in the Kamnitz hotel, we drove a little way out of the town to visit an excellent agricultural school for boys, which could take 250 pupils, but now has only 90. They have found that many boys, after being trained, emigrate, mainly to America. Now they will only take boys who undertake to live in the Jewish colonies in Palestine when they are trained. We then drove to Tel Aviv, the suburb of Jaffa where the middle-class Jews live. It is quite new, and well-planned, like a garden city, with clean paved streets, and all the houses painted white. The names of the streets, and all public notices,

15

are written in Hebrew. We visited the Gymnasium, a large building, the money for which was given by the Jewish Mayor of Bradford. After lunch at the hotel, we drove to the station, to take the train to Jerusalem. Huge crowds were there, and we had to fight our way in. After a very hot journey of four hours, we arrived at Jerusalem, and had to fight our way again to get out. Great crowds of pilgrims and visitors come here for Easter and Passover, and very many steamers arrived today. We drove to the East Hotel. As our luggage hadn't arrived, we couldn't dress for dinner, so had it in our private sitting room. Yellin came in later to tell us that the American Ambassador to Turkey, Mr Morgenthau, who is a Jew, is staying at the same hotel, and had invited us to join his party next day to go to Hebron, and visit the Mosque built over the Cave of Macpela, which normally none except Moslems may enter.

7 April A large party of us left at 7 in the morning, to drive in carriages to Hebron. The American Vice-Consul, Mr Edelman, also a Jew, came in our carriage. He was responsible for all the arrangements for the Ambassador's visit, and was rather anxious in case anything should go wrong. Also in the party were Dr Bliss, the head of the American Mission College in Beirut; his daughter and son-in-law, Mr and Mrs Dodge; Dr Robinson, an archaeologist from America; Dr Hodkiss, from Pittsburgh University; Mr Whiting, from the American Colony in Jerusalem; Lord and Lady Bryce; Mrs and Miss Morgenthau; and a few others. The Morgenthaus are very nice and friendly. We had two soldiers riding in front all the way. We had the Vice-Consul's 'kevass' on the box of our carriage—a sort of orderly, dressed in fine Turkish clothes with a long sword. The flowers by the side of the road were lovely: red anemones, blue irises, cyclamen and many other kinds. It was very hot.

About an hour's drive from Hebron we were met by a carriage containing the Hebron Chief Rabbi, and later a small troop of mounted soldiers joined us. It is a great event in Hebron for a non-Moslem to be allowed to enter the Mosque, and the authorities were taking no chances. The Ambassador received his permit direct from the Sultan of Turkey. Great crowds were there to see us arrive, and the flat roofs of the houses were covered with women, wearing white robes, and, of course, with their faces veiled. We drove under a triumphal arch, with a welcome written in Hebrew, and decorated with the trappings from the Synagogue, surmounted by the American and Turkish flags. We left the carriages, and entered a Jewish hotel where we went upstairs and on to a balcony. Crowds of Jewish children were gathered in the road, waving flags and singing Hebrew songs. We talked to the Chief Rabbi and his wife—she was an old West Central Club girl. Then we entered the carriages again, to drive to the Mosque. We were fully guarded by police and soldiers. As we entered the Mosque, they made a solid line behind us, as a precaution. The Moslems of Hebron are fanatics, and they muttered what seemed like threats, and looked extremely fierce. We saw the tombs of Abraham and Sarah, of Isaac and Rebecca, and of Jacob and Leah. We had passed the tomb of Rachel, by the side of the road, not very far from Jerusalem. We had had to take off our shoes to enter the Mosque, and walk in our stockinged feet. It was not such a beautiful Mosque as those we had seen in Cairo, but the biblical traditions, and the fact that we were so privileged, gave it great interest. As we left the Mosque, the crowds charged down upon us, and had to be forced back by our guards.

We returned to the Jewish hotel, where the Chief Rabbi read a lengthy address, and we all had lunch before returning to Jerusalem. On the return journey the weather changed. It became very cold and rained.

In the evening we went to a large dinner-party, given by the Ambassador, at the Jewish hotel, the Kamnitz, opposite the Fast. All the Hebron party were there, except the Bryces, as well as the Governor of Jerusalem and the Mayor (both Moslem), and the heads of many of the Jewish institutions in the town. The object of the dinner was to bring together people who usually quarrel with each other, and make them see each other's point of view. The Jews here seem a bigoted, narrow-minded and very difficult lot of people—no wonder Moses took 40 years to bring them through the wilderness if they quarrelled then as much as they do now. Their great quarrel today is whether Hebrew or German shall be the

17

language of the schools. The two sides just don't talk to each other.

I sat, at dinner, between the Mayor of Jerusalem and the American Vice-Consul. The latter told me that, for certain, Palestine was soon coming under French jurisdiction. But the Mayor said it was definitely going to remain with Turkey, and that the Turkish government were unable to make any reforms until the European Powers left them alone, and stopped being friendly in public, and treacherous behind their backs. After dinner Dr Robinson, the American archaeologist, told me that an English battleship had been making investigations off Jaffa, and that three hundred sheikhs of Palestine had petitioned Kitchener to take over the country and run it together with Egypt, and that this was likely to happen. Were they all pulling my leg? There were fifty people at the dinner: the Ambassador, the Governor and Dr Bliss all made speeches.

8 April A German Jewess, Mrs Myer, called, to ask mother's help in founding a school for girls. She said it was impossible to come to any agreement between the Zionists—the Hebrew speakers—and the Hilfsferein, the pro-German.

I'm disillusioned by Jerusalem. There are many religions here, but no religion. It is not only the Jews who quarrel. Moslem soldiers guard the Church of the Holy Sepulchre, to prevent the different Christian sects from attacking each other. We visited the church this morning, much to the horror of the British Consul, whom we called on later. He said that the Christians object to Jews entering their church, and if they knew we were Jews, it might lead to a row. And he said the Moslems were as bad about their Mosques, and that they had killed an American woman a few years ago for laughing in the Mosque of Omar, and now all Europeans have to go there with an escort.

The whole town is filthy, and many of the people, of all religions, look diseased and degenerate. I think it's more like the 'City of Dreadful Night' than the Holy City.

We lunched with the Yellins, and the Morgenthaus and Edelman were there, as well as Mr and Mrs Cowen, Zionists from London. Afterwards we all visited the Evelina de Rothschild school whose head, Miss Annie Landau, is a very live person. It was actually holiday-time, but she had collected the girls together for the day. It was very interesting. In the lower classes the girls talk Hebrew and learn English as a second language: in the upper classes, everything is in English. Their health is well looked after. An American woman, Miss Leon, runs a kind of District Nurse organization, known as 'the American Daughters of Zion', and one of these nurses visits the school, as well as a dentist, and there is a specially fitted-up room for them. There is a technical class for the older girls, where they learn embroidery, lace-making and fine needlework. There is also a class for defective children. Miss Landau and two other teachers come from London— one is from Commercial Street school and knew Alice and her work there. Later, we went to the house where Miss Landau lives with some of her teachers. Girls from the school learn cooking and housework there. Some of the older girls performed a Turkish play for us.

9 April Mr Yellin took us sightseeing in the old city, and to Mount Zion. We had coffee with Mr Valleiro, a rich banker. We walked all round the Jewish quarter in the old city. I feel somehow ashamed when I see such poverty-stricken Jews, many of whom are beggars, as if in a way I'm responsible. When I see the poor Moslems, I'm just interested, as an outsider. We went to the Bezalel art and craft school, and saw some Jews from the Yemen working there. Later, we picked up a guide, a sort of dragoman, to come with us for the rest of our tour, to the Lebanon and Syria too. He was a Jew from London, born in Duke Street, Aldgate, and educated at the Jews' Free School, at the same time as Israel Zangwill. He went to America, and became a sea-pilot, and then came to Jerusalem with his father, who left him money on condition he stayed there.

Then we went up the Mount of Olives, to call on Sir John and Lady Gray Hill. He is an elderly lawyer from Liverpool, who lives here half the year. He was very nice to us, showing us his lovely garden, and on to the roof of his house, with a view of Jerusalem on one side, and of the Dead Sea and the Jordan on the other. Lady Gray Hill is a game old lady, who paints pictures of the east, and has travelled with her native servants through Sinai, and even to the Sahara. We had tea with them, and then drove on to see a Russian church.

In the evening, a number of people called on us. We don't seem to get much time to ourselves. The Morgenthaus have now left Jerusalem.

10 April We were called for by Mr Myhus, Yellin's brother-in-law, and went with him in a carriage to see the Nebi Moussa procession, when the chief sheikh carries the Holy Flag from the Mosque to what the Moslems regard as Moses' grave, near the Dead Sea. There were huge crowds by the sides of the road, Moslem families with their children, enjoying the sunshine. We waited for about two hours near the Virgin's tomb, watching various lively processions. One consisted of a solid phalanx of men, with a man we were told was a dervish walking on their shoulders and waving a sword. There was a maddening sort of music from tom-toms, and men chanted, and waved sticks. One group of dervishes danced about wildly, and seemed to stick knives into themselves. We were told that the chief sheikh was in the Mosque, and mustn't be disturbed, and that he probably wouldn't appear for some time. It was terribly hot, and we thought it might be cooler driving so we drove down the Jericho road till we reached the Governor's tent, full of the town notables. The Mayor came out to greet us, and said he would have liked to have asked us to come into the tent, but no women were allowed inside, so we drove back, and waited under the shade of the city wall. At last, guns were fired, to show that the sheikh had left the Mosque, and the main procession came by, some on horseback, and the chief sheikh carrying the Holy Flag. They stopped opposite the Governor's tent, and he blessed the flag, and the procession went on.

Driving back, we saw a man we were told was a Christian who had insulted the flag stabbed by a soldier, and bleeding severely from his head and arms. He was dragged along in the dust by the soldiers, and each time he stopped, they hit him with their rifles. Father insisted on stopping and putting him into our carriage, to take him to the hospital, while we walked on. We heard later he had died.

In the evening we went to the Seder Night service at the Yellin's house.

11 April Jerusalem is more full of tourists and pilgrims than it has ever been before. It was much emptier for the two years previous, because of the war with Tripoli. All the hotels and hospices are full, and people are sleeping in tents outside the walls. We saw a piece of ground where they plan to build a new hotel.

We walked through the Jewish quarter to lunch with Rabbi Horowitz. Being a Saturday, the orthodox Jews were flocking to the Wailing Wall, dressed in their long velvet coats of purple and red, wearing velvet hats with fur borders. Picturesque, but hot even to look at. It was a fiercely hot day. Lunch lasted nearly two hours, and consisted of many courses, including two of meat and two of pudding. A young man, Dr Newman, who had been educated at the American College in Beyrouth, was there. He is kept by a philanthropic society to work among the Jewish poor. There were also a young Hungarian Jew, and an ardent Zionist from Germany. Later, we visited the American Colony, which was started 33 years ago by Americans who had come to lead a communal life, and do good works, and were later joined by Swedes. In the evening, a second Seder service at Miss Landau's.

The next day we went to Bethlehem, and again saw Moslems guarding the Holy places in the Church of the Nativity, to keep the Christian sects from fighting each other. Later, we visited the Shara Zadeh Hospital, a clean, well-kept place, limited in the number of in-patients they can care for by lack of funds. It was very orthodox: Dr Wallach, the doctor in charge, refused to shake hands with a woman! The following day we drove to Jericho, in a carriage with three horses, on a very bad, rocky road. We were accompanied by our dragoman, Captain Goldstein. We had to take all our own food with us, as it was Passover, and there was no Jewish hotel or restaurant in Jericho, an entirely Arab little town. We found Jericho extremely hot, but very attractive. We drove, later, to the River Jordan, through the wilderness of Judea. Except round the Dead Sea itself, the land looked as if it could be very fertile, if

21

well cultivated. But it all belonged to the Sultan of Turkey, and was uncultivated, only covered with thorny scrub and masses of brilliant yellow marigolds. My diary goes on:

The Jordan is a very pleasant surprise, looking just like the Thames, with luscious green shrubs and overhanging trees. We saw the Russian pilgrims bathing in the river. Hundreds of them come to Palestine each year, and the Russian government helps them pay for the journey, and has built large hospices where they stay. They walk, literally, in the footsteps of Christ, and buy holy shrouds, in which they bathe in the river, and then take home with them to be buried in. We passed groups of them walking from Jericho to the Jordan, looking painfully hot in the clothes they wore, which were more fitted for the Russian winters.

We then drove, through barren land, to the Dead Sea, which is a tremendous surprise when approached from the north, as one suddenly comes upon it from its own level. I paddled in it—it tastes bitter, and everything around is covered in salt.

It was quite cool in the evening, and we dined pleasantly in the garden of the Jordan hotel. A large party of wealthy-looking French pilgrims were in the hotel, and were very lively and rowdy—as were the jackals, the hyenas, the native tom-toms, and various shots in the dark.

Next day, after visiting old Jericho and the pool of Elijah, we returned to Jerusalem. During the Passover week, all our food was sent in from the Jewish hotel opposite, and eaten in our private sitting room. The day after, it rained violently. We visited a place called 'Abraham's Vineyard' to the north-east of the city, where two English philanthropists, Mrs Dunn and Mr Finn, run a small horticultural scheme for poor Jews—without any desire to convert them to Christianity.

We also called at the house of a rich Jew from Bokhara and found him, his wife and daughters all dressed in gorgeous-coloured robes. He showed us his collection of old manuscripts, Persian jewels, embroideries and so on. We walked back to the hotel through the very poor Mea Shorim Jewish quarter. In the evening, Miss Landau had a big dinner and reception in our honour.

The next day, we visited the Nathan Strauss Health centre, and were shown round by an American doctor, who later took us to his house to see his collection of amulets. Later, we went to the state prison, as one of Miss Landau's teachers wanted us to see the conditions under which her brother was living while awaiting trial for a murder of which, she said, he certainly was not guilty. He was in a kind of cage, together with his brother who was allowed in to keep him company.

My father was very anxious that the many Jewish charities working in Jerusalem should unite, and form some kind of Charity Organization Society. A large number gathered to hear what he had to say, at the Kamnitz Hotel. They formed a Committee, with Mr Valleiro, the banker, as chairman. As I wrote in my diary, 'whether it will be any good is uncertain'. Unfortunately, I was right.

We went to the Garden of Gethsemane, and to the Wailing Wall, where I was impressed by the earnest behaviour of the Jews who were praying, both men and women, despite the number of tourists who were watching them. We had a look at the Karaite synagogue, and called in at the Bikur Holim Hospital. The doctor in charge had invited us, and urged we should let him know the exact time of our visit. We could easily understand why.

As I wrote in my diary:

The building is bad, but they hope to have a new one. The sheets were dirty and food-spotted, everything was covered with flies, remains of meals were lying about, some of the patients lay in bed with their clothes on, the place outside the lavatory stank, and leading from it were two tiny rooms, each for two people. There was only one trained nurse—the Matron—but she was not there. The whole impression was of a dirty and badly organized place.

18 April We went to the Mosque of Omar with a 'kevass' from the British Consulate. It is one of the compensations of Jerusalem—I am gradually discovering them, and don't think it quite such a dreadful place as I did at first. The green and blue tiles covering it from the outside are so beautiful in the sunlight, and against the blue sky, I could have stood gazing for hours. Inside, with the sun shining through the stained glass windows, it was just as lovely. While we were looking at the rock where, traditionally, Abraham was prepared to sacrifice Isaac, we were told that, quite recently, some English officers had bribed one of the Mosque guards to be allowed to excavate under there for treasure. They were eventually discovered, and had to flee the country to save their lives. [Years later, I met one of the excavators, who was embarrassed that I should know of his escapade.]

I saw a Russian funeral today, for a woman pilgrim. I was standing on the hotel balcony, and I looked straight down on her face, as they leave part of the coffin uncovered till they reach the cemetery.

We leave tomorrow, and many people called to say good-bye. Although I wanted to get away from Jerusalem last week, now I am quite sorry to go. I hope to come back some day.

Next morning we left in a carriage, accompanied by Captain Goldstein, to drive north to Nablus. It took us about ten hours. We stayed at the Nablus Hotel, which belonged to a German tour company, HAPAG. It consisted of one large room, for meals, and four quite big rooms leading off it, each with four or more beds. Women slept in some of the rooms, men in the others, so I slept in the same room as my mother. The beds—as well as the food—were pretty bad. We visited the Samaritans, an old Jewish sect who only live in Nablus. We had been given a letter of introduction to the head of the community by David Yellin, and he showed us their holy writings, rather different from Hebrew, and over a thousand years old. There is a lack of girls in the community, and, through an interpreter, the chief Samaritan tried to persuade me to stay behind and marry one of the superfluous young men!

The Arabs of Nablus are as fanatical as they are in Hebron. Captain Goldstein, who had been wandering round the town on his own, came in late, very worried. He had no permit to carry fire-arms, but all the same had a pistol in his pocket, which had fallen out and been seen. He urged us to start very early in the morning to escape consequences, so we left before seven am. We arrived at Zichron-Jacob, a Jewish 'colony' on a spur of Mount Carmel, about nine hours later, after driving through lovely country full of wild flowers. Norman Bentwich had a married sister who had settled with her husband two years earlier in the colony, and built a house there, and made a delightful garden. Unfortunately, they were away, so we stayed in the somewhat primitive 'Graffe Hotel'. There were about a thousand people in the colony, mainly Romanian, and they employed Arabs from neighbouring villages to do the hard work. Next day we met the Aaronson family: Aaron, the eldest brother, had discovered a form of wild wheat which is disease-resisting; we visited his experimental agricultural station on the coast road, below Zichron. We were told he possessed the only car in Palestine and that he could drive it down the hill to the station, but often had to employ mules to pull it up again.

Next, we drove to Haifa, which we found an uninteresting town. My diary continues:

22 April We left the hotel at 5.15 am, to catch the train for Semakh, arriving there about 9. We went on a steamboat from there, across the Sea of Galilee to Tiberius—a most uncomfortable journey, as the boat was overcrowded with rowdy Germans. It should be hot here, as it's six hundred feet below sea-level. But today it is cold and wet. We stay at the Tiberius Hotel—along with the rowdy Germans. Two-thirds of the inhabitants of Tiberius are Jews, the rest Moslems. The town is not very interesting. In the afternoon, we took a sailing boat to the north of the lake, to see Kinnereth, where there is a farm school for girls as well as a small Jewish colony. Twenty girls are in the school which seems rather a slovenly sort of place. But they are having a new teacher soon. They grow fruit and vegetables and send them by train to Damascus. On our way back we stopped at an old synagogue to see the tomb of an old Rabbi, and to look at the sulphur springs and baths.

The next day, we first visited the tomb of the Jewish philosopher Maimonides—my father always liked seeing tombs—and then took a boat to the north end of the lake. At first, the men we engaged to row the boat went on strike, and said it was too far. They were greatly upset because the Turkish government had issued an order calling up all men between twenty and forty, and they feared another war. But when they had walked off, they discovered it was only for manoeuvres, and not for war, so they came back, and they took us at great speed, first to the place where the Jordan flows into the lake, and later to Capernium, where we saw the recently-excavated ruins of the old synagogue where, tradition has it, Jesus preached. An old German monk is responsible for the excavations which I found, in this setting, unusually attractive.

We returned to Semakh the next morning, and took the train to Damascus. A few years before our visit, there had been a damaging fire in the town, destroying part of the bazaars, which they re-built with corrugated iron roofs—safer against further fires, but less picturesque than the more primitive coverings. The streets were full of unattractive dogs, who acted as scavengers. The bazaar selling old clothes was popularly—and no doubt rightly—known as the 'louse market'.

We visited the place where Saladin and his vizier were buried, and nearby are the graves of two Turkish aeronauts, national heroes who crashed near Damascus the previous year. The situation of the town is beautiful—a large patch of brilliant green standing surrounded by barren brown earth. We went to see a Jewish school for boys, run by the French Alliance Israelite, situated in an old palace. We were impressed by the boys in the top form, who seemed highly intelligent, and were studying philosophy and science. We were taken there by a Jewish clerk from the bank where my father had cashed a cheque. He took us to see some very rich relations, who lived in a gorgeous, luxurious house, tucked away behind walls in a filthy street. The old head of the family was smoking a hookah, and talked only Hebrew. His granddaughters were dressed in the latest fashion, and had a French governess. We next saw two uninteresting synagogues and an appallingly bad kindergarten, where the children were extremely dirty, fifty of them were crowded into a room twenty feet by twenty, and the teachers were untrained girls. But they must provide something for the children, however bad, to prevent them going to the missionary schools.

27 April My mother and I had been invited by a Jewish woman in a shop to visit a Moslem home. We entered an enormous courtyard, full of oranges and lemons and roses, and went into a large room with thin alabaster windows. The man of the house has three wives, whom we met, as well as a number of his children. One girl of fifteen was already married, with a baby. The girls wore sloppy cotton frocks and jersey coats, and looked very untidy. The children were dirty, and begged for 'backsheish'. The beautiful rooms were used for cooking, dressing, and all domestic jobs. Squalor in luxury, as it were.

The Jews in Damascus are mainly very poor. We visited a brasswork factory, run by a Greek Christian, to provide them with work. He teaches them a trade, and pays them. There are six hundred workers, mainly girls, and many start at the age of three. It's really dreadful to see these tiny children carving the brass, when they can scarcely hold the tools, and doing the well-known 'Damascus' inlaid work on wood. One child of six was doing this beautifully. It seemed to be nothing but 'slave labour', but we were told many of the children were orphans, and this keeps them off the streets. We saw the shop where the products are sold—at a profit.

We had been invited to tea at the English hospital with Dr and Mrs Mackinnon. Lord and Lady Bryce were there, and a number of missionaries. It is a Scotch Presbyterian hospital and doesn't practise conversion. After dinner I went with Captain Goldstein to listen to the band playing outside the Government House. The crowds were quite orderly. Then we strolled through a closed bazaar, where men were drinking and gambling. Goldstein told me, rather naively, that this was the 'vice centre' of the town, and I mustn't tell my parents I had been there!

The next day we went by train to Baalbek, to see the magnificent ruins of the temples. The hotel was about the worst we had struck: they charged us quite a lot for bringing us some hot water to wash in. Then we went on by train to Beirut which we found featureless and unattractive, though the country round was lovely—and the hotel really good.

2 May Left on the *Saidieh* of the Khedivial Line. Goldstein very sorry to part with us, and presented us each with a bunch of flowers. When we thanked him, he grunted: 'They only cost fourpence.' Only one other English passenger on board, a few Americans, a lot of Germans and various odds and ends, including heaps of priests. We saw in the harbour the remains of the Turkish torpedo boats sunk by the Italians about two years ago. The bodies of twenty men are still there, it's said.

The captain of this ship is Greek, and the chief engineer British. There are very many cockroaches aboard—even in the sugar-basins on the table—and altogether it's not very clean.

We called at Larnaka [Cyprus] the following day. Fortunately, the sea was calm. We had deck cabins, but could not have our port-holes open, because natives camped on the deck outside, and the captain told us they were certainly verminous, and warned us against having the port-holes open. The cockroaches invaded the beds, especially under the pillows. On 5 May, we arrived at Smyrna, where we landed in small boats. The Khedivial agent there was a young Jew, who took charge of us, and showed us the town. It made a good impression, being clean and tidy. We returned to the ship, and rose next morning at 5, to see the passage through the Dardanelles. I was disappointed, as it was a wide passage, and not as I had imagined it would be, and it was extremely cold and cloudy. But when we saw Constantinople in the late afternoon, and the sun had appeared and was setting in a brilliant red sky, it seemed one of the most beautiful places I had ever seen. The head dragoman of the Chief Rabbi, Nahum, met us, looked after our luggage, and took us to the Pera Palace Hotel. The next day, accompanied by another Jewish dragoman, we drove to the Mosque of St Sophia which, though unattractive from the outside, is beautiful inside, being perfectly proportioned. Afterwards, we went to the Museum, before lunching at the American Embassy with the Morgenthaus, together with the Chief Rabbi and his wife. Later, we spent some very happy hours in the lovely bazaars.

During our five days of sightseeing in Constantinople, we were taken to see the Sultan go to the Mosque on the Friday. We were unimpressed. As I wrote:

He is a fat animal-man: they say he drinks—whisky and brandy as wine is forbidden to Moslems. He was in prison for thirty-two years. Nahum says he is quite pleasant to talk to.

28

Later, we went up the Bosphorus by train and boat to the American Girls' School, in order to see a Palestine girl from Richon-le-Zion, in whom Captain Goldstein was interested. We had tea with Mrs Murray, the principal. In the evening we dined with the Chief Rabbi and his wife: the Morgenthaus were the other guests. A man, Rousseau, whom my father had met on his business visit to Turkey in 1908, took us to lunch at a restaurant, together with Ismet Bey, a Turkish poet. Later, we went to the Ronssean house to see his children. I always enjoyed opportunities to see something (however little) of the life of the people of a country. Living in a hotel is so remote from real life. On 10 May the Morgenthaus lent us their car and a chauffeur, and we drove to Therapen, and all along the Bosphorus. The next day, we left for home, by train, travelling in the Orient Express for three days.

This long train journey was a comfortable, but unexciting, way of travelling. At Sofia we found the Chief Rabbi, who had heard we were on the train, and had come to meet us. My father left us at Brussels, to hurry home—and to avoid meeting Hugh, who was staying there. After spending three days with Hugh, we returned home, to be met—and questioned—by detectives on our arrival in England. They expected he would be with us, but were disappointed.

1914—1915

England

When war broke out Norman Bentwich was home on leave. I had spent a day with him in London, visiting the Law Courts, and his chambers in Lincoln's Inn. And he had suggested that, while I was staying at Chartridge, we should write to each other. As soon as war started, he was asked to help at the Treasury Solicitor's office in matters of International Law, which he did until he was recalled to Egypt, in November, much to his regret. I prefer to insert the actual letters, in most cases, as they give a truer picture of the time when I wrote them than if I paraphrased them today.

Chartridge
28.8.14

It's good of you to find time to write to me, when you are so busy. You say you wonder what I think of the war; I'm afraid my opinions are very childish, and pure Jingo. Because I think that the only thing to do is to concentrate on smashing Germany. I believe we're fighting for an ethical truth, and that the war is a struggle between civilization, and all it stands for, on one side, against Germany's barbarism, which seems the result of their extraordinarily rapid and material progress of the last forty years, which isn't based on any solid civilization. Fortunately, this war can be regarded as entirely brought on by German royalty and aristocrats, and while hating them, we can still feel pity for and sympathy with the people of Germany, who are forced to accept this tyranny from above. I don't think there is any real animosity between the common people of Germany and England, at least, not more than can be forgotten when the war is over.

You write about Zionism. I wish prominent Jews would stop writing about Jewish problems to *The Times* just now. They will only stir up Anti-Semitism among the Christians, and arouse the anger of the non-Zionist Jews. After all, we are only a very small proportion of an enormous empire, but some Jews seem to think we are the most important part of it. Why can't we forget our own particular interests and quarrels till the war is over?

If Russia would only treat the Jews as generously as she is treating the Poles, much of this Jewish nationalism would be unnecessary. I, personally, should never like to be a member of a Jewish State, and should always consider myself English if I had to live there. I think the ideal would be to use Palestine as a centre to make Jews, living in all countries, feel a common bond of brotherhood. Perhaps, by becoming a force for peace in the lands where we live, we really could be a force in the world.

I'm just existing as a useless female at present. There's nothing definite for us women to do. I've joined a Territorial Nursing Detachment in Chesham, and my friends are inclined to laugh at me for doing that.

Chartridge
8.9.14

If Turkey joins in the war, will there be trouble in Egypt? Perhaps, before long, we'll see Palestine under the British flag. This may make things more complicated for the Zionists out there. It will undoubtedly ensure material well-being for the people of the country, but it will surely be more difficult to establish Jewish thought and culture in a Christian-run country than in a Moslem one. And possibly the country would be 'run' by those English Christians who are already trying to undermine Judaism there. However, it may not work out like that, and Palestine being under the British may act as a stimulus to the Jews here. Anyway, it would be a good thing for Zionism to remove the German influence which seemed so dominant when I was there.

Everyone says 'business as usual', and even you say that it's important to keep home interests and normal life running smoothly. I think most of the work which women are called on to do during the war is just drudgery. I'm wondering whether, if women had the vote, there would have been a war? I go up to London most days, just carrying on my work, visiting families for Lily's Club. Too many Jewish young men are not enlisting: they say it's not a living wage, and they won't go till they're made to. Of course, many are aliens, and wouldn't be accepted.

London
14.10.14

A colossal muddle is developing over 'Relief Work'. It is chiefly due to trying to run Committees with titled inexperienced women together with representatives of the women's trade unions and experienced social workers. The resultant mixture of old-fashioned charity and an attempt at socialism is really comic. I see it at the Club, where we have 1,000 girls working now, all of whom would be otherwise unemployed. We're not allowed to take private orders for the garments they are making; it all has to go through a central committee. The girls are paid Trades Board wages, and have to be given money for their dinners, and needn't have free meals if they don't want to. And we have to take any girls the Labour Exchange sends us—that is all Socialism. On the other hand, we have voluntary helpers and voluntary cutters-out, and typists and register-keepers—when of course we could easily find out-of-work professionals for these jobs. And if there isn't enough work for the girls, they have to have lessons—from amateurs, including me—and receive their wages all the same. Meanwhile, work which should come to the workrooms is being done by 'patriotic ladies' in cosy little suburban groups.

Our workrooms at the West Central are such a muddle, we are closing them down next week, and starting one, without any public funds, just for the girls of the Club. It was all done in such a panic—and Queen Mary was involved—because, if things were properly organized, there are heaps of workshops which could have been turned over at once to making uniforms and equipment for the troops.

32

We've four Jewish girls staying here who are refugees from Antwerp. They were born in Jerusalem, and attended the Anglo-Jewish school there; later, their father emigrated to Belgium as a diamond-cutter.

I heard from Norman that he was leaving for Egypt on 6 November, having been recalled. He asked me to meet him the day before. After having tea at the Carlton Hotel, we walked up and down Whitehall, with the searchlights playing overhead, and he asked me to marry him, and to go and live with him in Jerusalem when the war was over. I was completely taken aback, and unable to give him a definite answer. We parted at Charing Cross Underground station, with the understanding that I would give him an answer as soon as I had made up my mind. Meanwhile, we wrote long letters to each other, and I told nobody of his proposal. It was not until 10 March that I sent him a cable saying 'yes'. I think I knew all the time what the answer would be, but took long to decide, as I was daunted by the idea of living in Jerusalem. There was so much that I had disliked there when I visited it with my parents. We both blindly accepted the idea that living there was going to be possible after the war.

My letters became longer, and very frequent. In December, I was 'called up' by the Territorial Nursing Detachment I had joined, to go and work in a hospital in Aylesbury. My next letters are from there.

Aylesbury
16.12.14

I'm now here, working in a hospital which has been set up in a factory normally producing rivets—whatever they are. The hospital is for the men in the large camp at Halton, where Ellis is now a 2nd lieutenant in the King's Own Yorkshire Light Infantry. I'm billeted on an elderly maiden lady in a very nice house, in a small square in the town. She's very charming, and excessively kind, and seems to enjoy molly-coddling me. It's quite embarrassing the amount she expects me to eat, and the number of blankets and hot-water bottles with which she supplies me. She's very easily shocked, and went nearly black in the face when I told her about Hugh having been in prison. It's rather a temptation to exaggerate to someone like that.

She's very pious, and says grace before meals, and is one of those people who clinches every argument with 'Well, but if you believe in God.' She makes me feel that if I disagree with her I'm one of the damned.

I work every morning in the Hospital, which is a mile from here, from 8 am till 2 pm. I've got my bike here with me. We've got to start by working in the kitchen, to get used to the 'discipline'. I feel I've never really worked in my life till now. Talk about 'menial occupations'—why, it's the hardest thing in the world to wash up properly, and clear away methodically, and peel potatoes skilfully, and carry things on trays without smashing them. It's humiliating to be such a duffer at it, because being educated ought to help, but the stupidest little skivvy girl can do these things instinctively, and I have to be taught how, and then do them badly. It's very difficult to carry a dozen basins of soup on a tray, without spilling any, when the Matron is watching me with a critical eye. She's really very nice, but an awful dragon, and won't let me be one minute without doing something. Her motto is: 'When in doubt, wash up.' It seems such a waste of time, when everything is dirty again a few minutes later. I get very tired, and my old lady sends me to bed early. I have my bath to the strains of the 'Last Post', as there is a detachment of the Oxford and Bucks Light Infantry across the square.

I've been reading Selma Lagerloff's *Jerusalem*. Her descriptions of the City make it more real to me than anything has done since I was there. Thinking of Palestine, I feel that the life in the Jewish colonies there is too separate from the life in Jerusalem itself. It seems like a segregation of those Jews who live in modern, up-to-date villages from those who live in poverty and squalor in Jerusalem, Hebron and Tiberius. Is a Jewish Palestine eventually to be like the modern colonies—or like the decaying towns? If Zionism could weld these two together, they might produce a really great State. I've never got over the shocked feeling Jerusalem gave me.

Aylesbury
30.12.14

You must have been having stirring times in Egypt, with the

34

removal of the Khedive. Is the new one as splendid a person as *The Times* makes him out to be?

The War Office has ordered that all those working in the hospital shall be inoculated against typhoid, and now I have a temperature, and my old lady insists on my staying in bed. Last night I woke screaming, because I dreamt I was being chased by the faceless lepers of Jerusalem. I still do washing up and peeling potatoes at the hospital, and it's extraordinary how much I'm now enjoying it. Did you read an article in *The Times* one day last week of the 'Temptations of Simplicity'? It said that many people were finding it a tremendous relief to have really simple routine-work to perform, such as soldiering or nursing, instead of the normal responsibilities of civilian life. That's exactly what I feel. I'd like to chuck all my work in London, which is never as satisfactory as it should be, and stay here as kitchenmaid.

The sergeant has been drilling his men just under my window, in the square. My education in 'military language' is being much improved, though I thought I knew quite a lot before. To counteract it, I've been reading Meredith's poems, which I love. I envy you your job of censor; it has always been the one ambition of my life to be able to read other people's private letters. I suppose the pleasure wears off after a time. This is the first time I've actually lived away from home, and the first time I've eaten unkosher food, and ridden on the Sabbath. While I was at home, I kept the observances to please my parents, but never saw any sense in them. Do you think that, if Palestine ever became the Jews' National Home, they would be able to codify the observances, and have as few as possible essential ones, and leave the rest to individuals to do as they like?

Aylesbury
14.1.15

I've started to work in the wards now, after a longer time than usual in the kitchen. I'm told the Matron almost despaired of me, because of my inefficiency. Once she saw me sitting down to peel potatoes, instead of standing at the sink, and was heard to say: 'Is that girl as mental as she seems?' Why shouldn't I sit to peel potatoes, and rest my weary feet? I always behave

35

extremely well at the hospital—the uniform makes me look demure, like a Sunday-school teacher, and it influences my conduct. I enjoy making new friends, though some of the girls there are from round Chartridge, and old friends.

My old billet lady is becoming rather a trial. She's so awfully good to me, that I feel a horrid beast because I'm not half grateful enough. But she *is* so *Cranford* I feel a complete anachronism in the house.

I've been reading a story of Hardy about a man who marries a girl simply on the strength of the letters she writes him, only to find out she is an illiterate servant-girl, and the letters were written by her mistress. Actually, I *am* writing my own letters, but you'll discover that very often in one letter I disagree with what I said in the one before. It's because I jump at conclusions, and foist them off on you as weighty opinions. So, when we meet, you mustn't ever chide me because I don't agree with myself.

Aylesbury
5.2.15

I'm now on night duty, from 8 pm until 8 am, and sleep in the day-time. They're short of people willing to do this, so, being young and strong I thought I should volunteer. We've a most interesting set of men in the hospital, and I've more time to talk to them than in the day-time. They're all 'Kitchener's Army', and have had such varied careers before: mostly they're the kind of people one doesn't meet in ordinary life. We've a sailor from a tramp steamer, an oil-borer from Mexico, a stevedore, a half-Chinese clerk from a Shanghai tea-firm, many coal miners and iron smelters, navvies, waiters, and a professional footballer, among many others. The half-Chinese clerk has come in for something wrong with his inside, and the doctor, looking at him, wrote it down as jaundice. Last night this lad said to me: 'Nurse, should I tell the doctor it's not jaundice making me yellow? You see, it's because I'm half Chinese. I'm really quite all right, although he keeps saying I'm not a proper colour yet. I'm getting bored here with nothing to do, so would he mind if I told him?' I told him of course he must, so tomorrow he's going to confess.

The extraordinary thing about the men is that they take no

interest at all in the war. They'll dash at the papers as soon as they arrive in the morning, and if I ask what the news is, they'll answer: 'News? We're sick of the war. We only look at the football.' Football is the common bond among them, from wherever they come. There was great indignation one day when they read that some man who is one of the best forwards somewhere in the North had enlisted. 'What does he want to spoil the team for?' was the general comment. One might think that, having enlisted themselves, they'd be furious with those who are still playing games. It's obvious that the papers don't represent the opinions of *these* men when they write of 'slackers' still playing football.

I'm writing this at the hospital, because there's really little to do at night. It's now 2 am, and it's queer that all the men seem to wake up together about this time, so I must stop, and go round giving them their medicines, and gargles, and drinks of milk. This makes me feel I've really the status of a nurse!

Aylesbury
12.2.15

When I write long letters to you on night-duty, I get told off in the morning by the Matron because the spoons aren't thoroughly clean, or the bread has been wastefully cut. It's ridiculous, but at 5 am I wake the poor Tommies, wash them, make their beds, and given them their breakfast. They always grumble at being woken up so early, when they've nothing to do all day. I find it's bad enough when I'm going to be busy.

The worst part of being down here is that all the people amongst whom I live and work are so extraordinarily unintelligent. There are five girls at the hospital with whom I'm very friendly, and not one is interested in good books, or intelligent subjects. And it's the same with the older women, too. And as for my billet-lady! *She* spends her leisure-time knitting and thinks it wrong to read novels while our brave men are fighting in the trenches. She never reads anything except Church papers. I called her a Pharisee in the course of discussion the other day, and she didn't like it. I didn't mean to be rude. I thought people *liked* being Pharisees. She is always lecturing me about my 'duty', and when I say I prefer to do just as I like, she says the modern young person is going to perdition, because it pays no attention to its elders. I hate being called 'a modern young person.' I want to be unique! She and I have long talks on the State Endowment of Churches, Tithes, Clergymen's salaries, and similar subjects I've never thought about before. It's fun to jump to conclusions on things I know nothing about, and then foist them off on her as weighty opinions, worthy of argument. She takes me so seriously; but sometimes, when I'm actually ragging her, she looks at me over her spectacles and says, 'My dear child, I do believe you are pulling my leg.' Then I hastily assure her that is the last thing on earth I'd ever do. It's queer, living for the first time entirely in a world of Christians. I find some of them so intolerant and narrow-minded about Nonconformists and Roman Catholics. It seems so un-Christian, and so unlike what they're taught in the New Testament. I love reading it, especially Luke and Revelations. The ideas are put so simply, and one can see how the renegade Jews were stirred into religious fervour by the language and parables they could easily understand. When I hear anyone being anti-semitic, I long to remind them that Christianity came into being because their forbears were irreligious, and had to be reformed by a new religion. And that *my* ancestors didn't need the new religion.

I must stop now. The night-sister is calling me, because I expect she's discovered all those plates I've not yet washed up.

Aylesbury
29.2.15

I'm sorry I can't send you a photograph, but I've never been taken since I was a child. There have been such heaps of scathing letters in the papers, and articles, about girls who only do nursing for the sake of the uniform, that I'd scorn to be ranked among them.

I'm feeling gay tonight, as it's my last night on duty, and then I return to normal hours. But I'm afraid I'm being de-graded, and put back in the kitchen for a week, before I go home on a week's leave, and return later to the wards again.

I'm sending you something I've written about my work here. I often try to write, with consistent lack of success in having anything published. You, who have already had books

38

Helen Bentwich as a child at Chartridge with her father and Ellis

Helen Bentwich's mother

published, won't know the sickening, squashed sort of sensation one feels when an envelope in one's own handwriting appears, and a neat little 'declined with thanks' slip falls out with the returned manuscript. Anyway, I really am now a successful kitchen-maid, even if I'm a complete failure as an author.

I went home on leave early in March, and after a few days, I longed to be back there. But measles had broken out, so they told me to stay at home until they needed me again. Meanwhile, I had promised Norman I would marry him, so when I received a notification that, if I wished to continue as a member of the Nursing Detachment, I must sign on for the duration of the war, and be prepared to go to any part of the world where I might be needed, I regretfully decided I was unable to sign. I felt I must be at home, ready to marry him, if he were able to obtain leave. So ended my not-very-glorious career as a nurse in England.

I soon got in touch with the Guides again: there were now some three hundred of them in Whitechapel, and I was asked to become organizer for East London, which meant a certain amount of work. I took to going to tea with the mothers of the girls in my own Company, because I found that much more satisfactory than 'visiting' them as a social worker. We then talked as hostess and guest, and I learnt much about their lives in Russia or Poland, as well as of their day-to-day problems. I found it sad that there was so often a gulf between these Yiddish-speaking parents and their English-educated children, and I did what I could to bridge the gulf among my particular girls.

I had to organize a rally and competition for all East London Guides, at the People's Palace, in Stepney, one Saturday. It would not have been popular to have ridden there on the Sabbath, so I stayed the night in a small flat in College Buildings, near Toynbee Hall, which my sister Alice rented to make her eligible to stand for the Borough Council at the next election. The only water for five flats was from one tap on a half-landing. Baden-Powell, the Chief Scout, attended the rally. It was 9 pm when he rose to speak to the girls and their parents. He told them how much he admired their good show of 'First Aid', and how useful they would be in air-raids. He added that he had heard that five Zeppelins were already on their way over to London. It was curious that he should have done such a tactless thing. The parents immediately made a dash for their daughters and raced home with them, and in a remarkably short time the hall was empty. The East End did not like to be out in Zeppelin raids, of which there were beginning to be quite a number.

My mother had, since the early days of the war, given hospitality to Belgian refugees. Now, when I was back living at Porchester Terrace, I found she had three, from Namur—an elderly woman, a Marchioness, who was a dignified and charming 'grande dame'; her married daughter, a Viscountess, a frivolous society woman, who spent her time playing bridge, and complained at the lack of gaiety in our home; and *her* seventeen-year old daughter, a nice, sensible girl, who during these weeks became my special charge. Through them we met Belgian officers and soldiers, who came to our house, and heard terrible accounts of the suffering in their country. Curiously, while I was working in Aylesbury, I was able, like the Tommies, to forget the war. But now that I was back in London, with no definite war work to do, once again I was aware of the horror and futility of it all. And, at this time the war had been extended to the Dardanelles, and many men I knew were sent there.

I resumed family visiting for the West Central Club. I found that Lily had marked me down as a future 'Club Leader', and often talked to me of what I could do for the Club after the war. I felt in a false position about this, and had to tell her, as soon as I'd cabled to Norman accepting to marry him, that I would be living out of England, and would be unable to work with her any more. Many of my more conventional relations seemed almost hurt at my engagement having happened without their being able to gossip about it beforehand. It took them entirely by surprise. As we had, between us, ninety-five aunts, uncles and first cousins, it was as well we had decided to live out of England.

After we were engaged, I wrote Norman copious letters, almost every day. But they were mainly concerned with what I thought, and read, because I was not actually doing anything worthwhile or interesting. Occasionally I would vary my visiting for the Club by a day with Alice, visiting for the Care Committee there. But I was not very happy doing that. I seemed to have to ask the kind of questions I should have resented being asked had I been the person questioned. In the evenings I undertook to organize all the classes for the foreign girls at the Club, which kept me busy.

I wrote and thought a lot about Palestine, and I mentioned in one letter that I was surprised to find my uncle Herbert Samuel was beginning to take a very great interest in Palestine. He had never seemed to care to hear much about it before, and was rather bored when we told him about our visit there in 1914. But, in the spring of 1915, he asked my father a great many questions about our visit there, and met Norman's sister and her husband, Nita and Michael Lange, who had lived there in a house they had built at Zichron-Jacob for two years. I wrote, for the first time, about the Hebrew University; and commented on the controversy raging in the papers round Israel Zangwill. I also wrote much about the labour problems in England, the various strikes, and the Trade Unions and my opposition to the 'pacifism' of the ILP. And I remarked how depressed everyone was about the war, and how they resented that bad news was so often withheld from us, and we often heard of disasters for the first time from men home on leave.

My mother thought it a good idea that I should learn something of domestic science, so I enrolled for a course at Berridge House in Hampstead, early in April. But I soon found it boring, and for the first time discovered the fascination of Hampstead Heath (where sixteen years later we made our home) and would lie there in the spring sunshine, writing to Norman, instead of learning how to make bread, or the theories of laundry work. One of the maids at Porchester Terrace, Esther, the under-parlourmaid, had asked if she could come abroad with us, after we were married, and take charge of our house. This seemed to me a much better arrangement than learning how to do it myself.

In May Norman's mother died, which cast a sadness over our happiness. They were a large and closely-knit family, and I had seen much of them since our engagement. He had nine sisters, and one brother, nineteen years younger than he was. His father, a lawyer, and editor of the *Law Journal,* was, like my father, an observant Jew, with somewhat old-fashioned ideas. But unlike my father, he was an ardent Zionist, and had been on what he called a 'pilgrimage' to Palestine some years before.

Norman came home early in July, and here is an extract from the last letter I wrote to him before we were married.

This has been an eventful day. First, your cable to say you'll be home in a fortnight. I was excited enough about that, and was sitting in my room writing to you, when my brother Cecil burst in to say he'd just become engaged to Kathleen Jessel, the daughter of Albert Jessel, who is a very charming and attractive girl. No sooner had he left my room, than Hugh came in, to tell me he'd been engaged for some time to Elsie Duval, the girl who had escaped to the continent with him, and he thought it was now time he made the engagement public. I know her, and like her very much. And all in the same evening as I heard you were coming home! It's like a badly constructed play. This is the last letter I'll write to you before we are married. I expect the censor will be glad our correspondence is over.

1915—1916

Cairo

We were married early in September, with the full regalia of a conventional white wedding, a guard of honour of the Girl Guides, and a reception in the garden of my home in Porchester Terrace. The recent death of Norman's mother, and the departure of my youngest brother Ellis that night for France, rather marred the joyousness of the occasion. Norman and I spent a quiet fortnight in Birchington as our honeymoon, and while there he received a cable recalling him to the Law School in Cairo. We spent many hours seeking permits to cross Europe, and take the ship from Marseilles. Esther came with us, because my mother realized that Norman would go off in the army as soon as he possibly could, and she said she would feel uneasy were I left entirely on my own in Cairo. Although I assured her this happened to very many girls, younger and less experienced than I was, I was extremely glad to have someone who would relieve me of the tedious business of house-keeping—especially as my mother paid Esther's fare.

Travelling in war-time was, of course, neither easy nor comfortable. After waiting four hours on the Boulogne boat at Folkestone, we had to transfer to another, as Boulogne harbour was said to be full of mines. So we travelled to Dieppe on the oldest and most overcrowded boat possible. There was nowhere to sit, so we camped on our luggage, and ate the food with which my mother had thoughtfully provided us. We arrived at Dieppe at 8.30 pm, taking six hours to get there; fortunately it was quite calm. It took another three hours to disembark, because of passport control. We have always worked on the theory that someone has to be last, and it might as well be us. So we slept on our luggage till all the passengers were off, and then got straight on the train, arriving at Paris at 4.30 am, and after again waiting for some time, found an ancient victoria with tired horses to take us to our hotel. We wanted to send a cable home to say we had arrived safely, but the post office refused it, and we had to take it to the police to be approved. In the end we sent it to my uncle, Herbert Samuel, the Postmaster General, and eventually they let that pass. We had an enjoyable day sightseeing in Paris, and took the night train to Marseilles. We stocked up again with food, and were pleased to find a shop where everything was done up in packets ready for a picnic. I'd never seen a shop like that in England.

Our ship, the SS *Caledonia* of the P & O Line, was delayed for twelve hours; so we spent the time sightseeing in and around Marseilles. The voyage was uninteresting, and the boat was overcrowded. I read Cromer's *Egypt*, to give me some background of the country. I also started to learn some Arabic, from Norman. We arrived in Cairo on 7 October.

Egypt, of course, was at that time under British control. There was the British Resident, with his staff. Until the outbreak of war this had been Lord Kitchener, now Minister of War, but in 1915 it was Sir Henry McMahon. The heads of all Government Departments were Egyptian, but each had a British Adviser, and many other Britons working with them, as in the Police, the Ministry of Education, Public Works, etc. Many of the judges, as well as the staff of the Law School, were British. As was customary in those days in places where the British were the 'ruling class', they tended to form their own society, which was the kind of society rapidly dying out in England, and one which I personally, had not come across before. During the months I spent in Egypt I never felt happy or at ease in this society, though I did my best to be acceptable, for Norman's sake.

The centre and core of this society, and I think the most harmful aspect of it, was the 'Sports Club', on the island of Gezirah, where most of the officials of the higher ranks lived. By and large this club was only open to the British, and no matter how educated and anglicized an Egyptian might be, he was a 'native', and not able to become a member. This social exclusiveness did more harm, and caused more dislike of the English, I believe, than anything else. It was Colonialism at its worst. The whole social life of the majority of the British community centred round this club and the 'Turf Club', in town, which was exclusively for British men, and where wives as well as 'natives' and dogs had to be left on the doorstep together.

Calling and being called on formed a large part of social life in those days, and the rules and taboos were as strict as in any society generally considered more primitive. A newly-arrived wife was called on by the wives of her husband's colleagues, and the heads of his department, as well as the wives of others who were his friends. All these calls had to be returned. Formal dinner-parties, where evening dress was always worn, were given for the newly-arrived wives, who then had to go through the ordeal of arranging the return parties. These parties were apt to be boring, as one met the same people over and over again, not in an informal friend-making atmosphere, but in the chilling formality of the carefully arranged dinners. At very, very few houses did one meet Egyptians, or even those highly educated Jews, Greeks, Italians, etc. who lived in Egypt and were lumped together as 'Levantines'. As the British community was large, it was usual for colleagues from the same Ministry to foregather. Fortunately for me, Norman had always been looked upon as a bit unusual in his disregard for some (though by no means all) of the conventions, particularly the friendships he had with Jewish families.

In the autumn of 1915 the Gallipoli campaign had begun to reach its most hopeless stage. Cairo was full of military, and seemed at that time to have an undue number of generals and staff officers. Most of them had their wives with them, but social mixing between the British civilians, living in their own settled homes, and the military, living either in hotels or furnished flats, was rare, certainly at our level. Esther, born in Knightsbridge Barracks, and the daughter of a well-known sergeant major, was immediately adopted by the military, and soon found a young man in the Lancers whom she eventually married.

Cairo at this time was a hot-bed of rumours, which flew around with astonishing rapidity. Matters were made worse because official news was withheld if it was in any way unpleasant. The hospitals were full of sick and wounded soldiers from Gallipoli, many of whom had been torpedoed on the way over, and only rescued after seeing their friends drowned. But we never heard the truth of these disasters, only the rumours, which sometimes became wilder and wilder in the telling. It was into this life, different from anything I had known before, that I plunged as soon as we arrived in Egypt. I wrote home to my mother at least twice a week, and she kept all the letters. Here are extracts from those I wrote as soon as I arrived.

Gresham House, Cairo

10.10.15

The weather is terribly hot, and the mosquitoes irritating. But not nearly so much as the Egyptian government. The Law School doesn't start for another month, and there was no need to send for Norman so urgently. The Head of the Law School, Mr Walton, had been told to get his English lecturers out, and he never warned Norman about the delay in opening, but instead told a woman who is running the Red Cross here that Norman would have heaps of time to work for her. Norman didn't like the idea of this, and is importuning the Ministry of Justice to see if there is anything he can do there. It's such a shame, as the Foreign Office at home offered Norman interesting work to do if he could stay on for a while. We are staying at Miss St John's pension, where Norman had a flat before, till we find one of our own. We had a lot of bother at Port Said with the customs over our large amount of luggage.

Cairo is full of soldiers, British, Australian and New Zealanders. I'm told there have been many more, but a number have been sent to Serbia, by way of Salonika, and of course many to the Dardanelles, because things are pretty bad there, and it's said that the officers are losing confidence in General Hamilton. People here say they are depressed about Bulgaria coming in against us; something must have gone wrong there. And there's a fear that Greece may do the same. I would like to find a job in a hospital, as I enjoyed working in the one in Aylesbury. But they are singularly empty now, and there's great competition, I'm told, to get taken on. When I've no regular work, I think too much about the heat. But I must start looking for a flat.

46

Norman is feeling happier, because he has been taken on at the
Ministry of Finance to do a temporary job, like the one he did
at the Treasury last month. And I'm doing some not-very-
inspiring work for a few hours each day at the Red Cross
office. Norman has a great friend here, Jack Mosseri, who
belongs to one of the rich Jewish families, and has an utterly
dog-like devotion to Norman. These Jewish families, however
well-educated, are looked on as 'Levantines' by most of the
population, and have little social contact with the British. We
went to dinner with the Mosseri family, and though Jack is
modern and European in every way, his mother is very
oriental. Arabic is her main language, although she does speak
Italian. We had some very queer things to eat, which she had
prepared herself. They live in a magnificent house, the sort
you go over with a guide in England, but it all seemed rather
dark and airless, and over-furnished. Being with a family like
this makes one realize one is in the east, and I think most of the
English want to forget that they are. Jack does a great deal of
social work among the poor Jews of Cairo. The Jews here
seem either extremely rich or very poor, although I expect
there are plenty in between whom one doesn't meet. He is
urging me to start Girl Guides among the girls in the Jewish
school. I must think about it.

We also called on another even richer Jew, Cattaui Pasha,
who lives in a still more magnificent house, which was
swarming with mosquitoes. And we've been down the Mousky—the bazaar. That was the part of Cairo I liked best when
we were here last year, and I know I'll go there whenever I
can. I learnt enough Arabic on the way over to ask for what I
want in it—but not enough to understand the answers. As you
know, I'm hopelessly bad at languages.

I've been out with a man who wants us to buy his little car,
and I'm driving it quite successfully. But Norman says we
can't afford it and must stick to bicycles. And we've found our
flat, and will move in as soon as it's ready. It's in a
newly-developed area, known as the Garden City, though as
yet it has no gardens. It's five minutes' walk from the
Residency, quite near the Nile, and the rooms on the one side

have a lovely view of the river, and there's a balcony on which I can sit and look at it. The other side looks out on the Citadel and the Mokattam hills. It's much healthier than living in the city. It has five rooms, and the rent is eight pounds a month. Mr Mandofia, the landlord, lives in the same building, and we fixed it up with him in five minutes. Miss Bailey, who is the nicest person I've met here so far, told us about it. She's in the Ministry of Education, and although actually she's the inspector of girls' schools, she is at present in charge of, and living at, the training college for girl teachers.

I believe in doing things quickly, so Esther and I have been shopping for kitchen equipment, and all the things which Norman hadn't got in his flat. It's amusing, because few of the shopkeepers talk English, though they can manage French. But as I don't know the French for all the pots and pans, etc. which I want, I just wander round the shop till I find what I'm looking for, and get it priced. But it takes time. A carpenter is making shelves and things like that, and the flat's being painted and whitewashed. We hope to be in after three days. It's the custom here, when anyone who comes from another country dies, or goes home, to have an auction in his house. And this, apparently, is a social occasion when all the late owner's friends meet and bid amicably against each other. We have been to an auction at the house of a man, Etherington Smith, who has recently died. We bought his piano, his very attractive dining-room furniture, some bedroom furniture which we need, a large meat safe, an ice-box, and a filter. The last is very necessary, as it's not safe to drink Cairo water unless it has been boiled or filtered.

We shall have a 'suffragi', as well as Esther, to run the house. A suffragi is a manservant from Berber, in the Upper Nile, is black, and dressed in a long white robe, like a nightgown, with a red band round his waist, and a red tarbush. He usually has a room on the roof, stays for a time, and then returns for a holiday to his family in Berber. All the suffragis in Cairo form a sort of club, and when you want one, you ask a reliable suffragi belonging to a friend to find one. The most expensive are marvellous cooks, but as Esther will cook, we shall only have a cheaper one. The one Norman had at Gresham House is a bad fellow. He was supposed to pack everything properly after Norman left, but he just put every-thing anyhow in the box-room, and lots of things are full of beetles and wood-lice, which here are great long things of peculiar nastiness. But the worst thing he did was to put the case of Norman's valuable International Law Books in the cellar without fastening it, and thirty of them have been stolen, just odd volumes of sets, no use to anyone except for the bindings. Norman is very upset about this, as he had a really good collection, which is now spoilt. One suffragi we thought of engaging demanded extra money for working for a woman, saying she expected more work from him than a man did.

I'm already getting tired of this wonderful sunshine. One of Norman's friends says that in Cairo the weather is lovely, but the climate is damnable. Think how limited one's conversation gets when all talk of the weather is superfluous! There is only one topic of conservation taking its place here, and that is people. Everyone talks of them for hours at a time, and I find it amusing when I meet new people whose family history, and character in all its facets, I already know quite well. Prices of some things are very high here. Coal for the kitchen stove is four pounds a ton. Potatoes are so expensive that people only have them for special occasions. And the eggs are so tiny that you have to use two where at home you would use one. I wonder if that is the climate or the wrong sort of chickens.

It's now Bairam, the Moslem religious holiday, when they eat nothing all day and feast all night.

Cairo
26.10.15

I've had a most interesting and pleasurable time going over Miss Bailey's training college. The college is free, but the children in the practising school adjoining pay six shillings a month. The students board at the college, and are fed and clothed free too. But they have to undertake to teach in government schools for two years when they are trained. They enter when they are 14 or 15, and stay for three years. There are 200 students. Some old sheikhs teach them Arabic, but Miss Bailey is trying to replace them. The college is divided in two parts, one for domestic training and one for ordinary education. There is an English teacher in charge of the domestic training side, and one for physical education, who comes from Dartford Physical Training College, and the rest are native. Most of the native ones have been over to England, to have their training in one of the training colleges there, some at the Froebel. The rest have only been trained here in this college. All the teaching is in Arabic. The college was started twelve years ago, but modernized fairly recently. The domestic training department compares favourably with any in England, and the gymnasium is much bigger than ours at St Paul's. It was interesting to see these Gyppy girls, who mustn't be seen outside without a veil, doing gymnastics in short cotton gym tunics. The rest of the time they wear different coloured overalls, according to the year they are in, with white veils on their heads, or caps for practical work. They are, in the main, from poor homes, because the upper-class families won't allow their daughters to come. This training makes them independent and able to earn their own living, and they won't marry at such an early age. The school was interesting too, but it was odd to hear English nursery rhymes sung in Arabic. All the dormitories are light and hygienic, holding about 70 girls each. And plenty of bathrooms. Of course, the school is only for girls. It's certainly one of the good things here.

It's queer that, while the men here are so anxious to ape western ways, it seems to make them have the worst qualities of east and west; yet with the girls this westernizing influence seems for the good. And anyway, why do the men want to try to be so western, and yet just those, of the upper classes, still want their women to remain completely eastern, in the harems?

I've now a bicycle. Riding it is quite effortless, as the roads are all so flat. Norman decided I must have one at once, after an incident which befell me, when an effendi—i.e. a European-dressed Egyptian—talked to me in a tram, waited for me outside the shop I went to, and was difficult to shake off. The next day when I went out, he was waiting for me again at the tram stop, so I bolted. He was quite unpleasant, and anyway, a bike will prevent this in future. I've been cycling down the Mousky, which must be unusual, as everyone stares and shouts. The Mousky is full of wounded soldiers buying presents for their nurses, or else to send home to their girls. I often get drawn in for my advice—but mainly they buy such awful stuff, and pay much too much for it. But it's hard to find anything worth buying now; the dealers have been doing such a roaring trade with the Australians, they are nearly sold out, and they're unable to import anything new from Persia or the Far East. So one can only buy things made in Egypt. I believe Cairo was never so prosperous as it is now.

Norman and Jack Mosseri are arranging to have a synagogue service for all the Jewish men in the army here, once a fortnight. Norman will run it, and give an 'address'. Some of it will be in English, as probably most of the soldiers don't know much Hebrew. And there will always be a friendly tea after.

Cairo

1.11.15

At last I've found a hospital which will take me on. It's the Kasr El Aini Hospital, normally the Government native hospital, but now taking a number of sick and wounded soldiers. I'm to do only half-time to start with. There are very few wounded patients, but very many with typhoid—it's a good thing I was inoculated. Some of the younger women's husbands or mothers won't let them go there, so that is why they have room for me. And there are dysentery patients, too, and others with other illnesses. It's quite unlike an English hospital. Originally it was a prison, then a barracks, and in Napoleon's time it became a hospital. It's the medical school for the Egyptians. All the walls are dark brown or dark red; the beds are very low, like stretchers, and the sheets are of unbleached calico, with red stripes, and so are the shirts and loose drawers which the Tommies have to wear. The native orderlies take the temperatures and pulses and give the patients their food. All the charts and prescriptions are written in Arabic, and I have to learn to talk to the orderlies in Arabic for anything I need. There is one British sister for three typhoid wards, of twelve patients each, and a morning help like me. It's right on the Nile, only a few minutes on my bike.

I was very scared the first morning, when I found I had to wash the typhoid patients all over, and change their sheets, because the only thing about typhoid I remembered from my Home Nursing lectures was that the patients mustn't be moved. And I stood there wondering what to do, till a very lively—but very ill—young Cockney said: 'Come on nurse, we'll show you what to do.' And they did. Only it's a bit back-breaking, making those low beds. I also have to prepare the milk-foods for them. I was rather shocked at first when I went into the large kitchen, and saw a pile of dirty sheets lying under the table, and an orderly sleeping on them. For all that, they are said to have the highest rate of cures for any hospital in Cairo. There's no silly etiquette about getting ready for the Doctor's rounds. The first morning I started getting flustered, like at Aylesbury when the Doctor came, but this one—an Egyptian—who came in followed by his students, told me, in English, just to carry on, and I felt it certainly was a good idea, because it meant that the patients were the first consideration, and not the Doctor. Birds fly in and out of the window all the time, and of course there are the flies. But all the same, it's most efficient and well-run. Some RAMC doctors supervise, but I've not seen any of them yet. And it's far more worth while than Aylesbury, where even making beds had to be done by two of us, and nobody was ever badly ill. Here all 'my' patients are on the danger list. I only hope the very nice sister doesn't discover how inefficient I really am.

I'm getting on quite well with the Girl Guides I've started at the Jewish school, and we are now registered as an Overseas Company. But they're a difficult lot. They're less interesting than mine in London; they cheat all the time, and whine when they lose. They seem to cram them with knowledge in the school, without bothering at all about developing their characters. They are very lively, a contrast to Miss Bailey's Arab girls, who just seemed to sit and talk in their play-time. These rush about and make a great noise, which is healthier.

Cairo
7.11.15

There are rumours that the Canal defences are in a poor condition and that 100,000 troops are being sent there. It seems true about a ship being submarined in the East Mediterranean, but it was a transport bound for Salonika and not a hospital ship, as you wrote. It went down in 10 minutes, but they managed to let down the boats. Ten New Zealand nurses were in the first to be let down, and the second fell on top of them, and they were all killed. And the soldiers and sailors were in the water eight hours before any were rescued. One hundred were lost, and many are in the hospitals in Cairo, including the one where I am working, wounded and badly ill from the results. By the way, although I tell you all this (and hope the censor will pass it), and honestly believe it while I'm writing it, I may have found out it's all only Cairo rumours before you get this. People here are such liars! On the other hand, I may at some time find out the truth from the men who have recently been brought into our hospital when they are well enough to talk. I'm in charge of one of the worst patients, just arrived from shipwreck—at least as to washing him, and changing his sheets, and preparing his food.

We met a nice couple at dinner the other night, the Quibells. He was Director of Antiquities at Sakkara, and is now the second man at the Cairo Museum. He was full of good stories, and told me of a village he had recently visited where all the inhabitants were Christians—Copts. They told him: 'This is a really Christian village. If any Mohammedan came and laid his prayer carpet here, we'd stone him.' He and I agreed it was a good definition of Christianity.

I've just heard another rumour. This time it is that Kitchener is on his way here, to have a look at the Canal defences. But the sceptics say it's only to look after the planting in his garden. It's funny with the Tommies in my hospital. They dread the thought of going back to Gallipoli, and long to go to France, looking on that as a sort of Elysium, where there are shops, and weeks out of the trenches, and a hope of leave.

Cairo

15.11.15

I came home unexpectedly a few days ago, and found our suffragi, with two friends, sitting at Norman's desk, carefully tracing out the 'character' one of them had on to our notepaper. I suppose he thought it was better than any that I would give him. Anyway he is now sacked, and we have a bright youngster of fifteen instead. We've been to the Zoo, which is in the garden of an old house of Ismael. They have some attractive beasts, including playful lion-cubs and monkeys.

But the most popular is Said, the hippopotamus, an enormous beast with a placid and unruffled expression, said almost to rival Kitchener in popularity. He is talked about as if he were a real person. And we've done a long walk, up to the Mokattam Hills, and down through the City of the Dead, where there are tombs each side of the road, instead of houses, and came out at the far end of the Mousky. When we came home the mail was in, with the papers. There's a strict censorship over bad news, I suppose because they think it's bad for morale for the natives to know when things go wrong. So we only see it in the home papers, or hear distorted versions in the rumours. And Norman gets depressed when he reads of the urgent appeals to men to join up, and all he has to do here is seven hours a week at the Law School, and six hours on a commission drawing up new codes of law. He goes around begging for more work.

It's quite fun at the hospital now. When I first went there, the men who were my special charge were all very ill indeed with typhoid, and groaning with pain and unable to move. But now they're all convalescing together, and are like a lot of schoolboys. They keep shouting for more food, and smoke all the time. They won't smoke the Egyptian cigarettes, and beg me to get them 'Woodbines', which are hard to obtain here, but Norman manages to get some. These men are so grateful and good-humoured, and so affectionate with each other, that it's really enjoyable being with them. They call each other by numbers, never by name, saying, 'Number Three is a jolly chap, ain't he?' or: 'Number One isn't half a caution.' But, in a room to himself, there's the man from the shipwreck, with double pneumonia, and on the danger list. He was in the water eight hours, until a New Zealander rescued him, and put him on a raft. His eyes are almost out of his head with fright; he must have seen some ghastly sights.

Cairo

20.11.15

We went to the Museum, which is marvellous, and while I was standing in front of some superfluous mummies which were for sale, Mr Quibell came up. I told him I was thinking of buying one—a lovely present to bring home—but he advised

54

The guard of honour after the Bentwich wedding, September 1915

1st Whitechapel Girl Guides leaving camp at Chartridge, August 1915

Reggie and the other test room men from Woolwich Arsenal, 1916

me not to, as they were inclined to smell a bit in amateur hands.

Jack Mosseri invited us to go out with him to a garden his family owns at Giza. Norman couldn't come, because he is examining for the Egyptian University on criminal sociology, in Arabic. It's amusing, thirty examiners are appointed by the Ministry of Justice for their knowledge of Arabic, and only two students. So Jack and I went alone, he, poor dear, being rather dubious about the propriety. The garden is right by the river, on a plot of land bought at the time when there was a boom in speculation, and never developed because then there was a smash. It had formerly belonged to the Sultan, the Red Palace, and they had bought it for £400,000, and have had it on their hands ever since; fifty acres of flower gardens, mango plantations, and date plantations, with this huge Red Palace, its harem and stables and all the rest of it. They just keep up the flower gardens, which are very fine, and a grotto, and a lake with a looking-glass at the bottom for the harem, and some gazelles. He told me to pick all the flowers I wanted, and I came back on my bike with a huge bunch of roses, sweet-smelling jasmine, narcissus and chrysanthemums. It's queer all these different kinds being in flower at the same time. The flowers look much nicer picked than growing, because unless they are continually watered they are always covered with dust—I suppose it's really sand. We picked and ate a lot of tangerines; and picked some loofahs from trees—things people use as sponges in their baths. And Jack has given me a permit to go there whenever I like, and sit there, and pick the flowers.

I've been down the Mousky with Mrs Walton to choose a wedding present from the Law School. We selected a very fine 14th-century Persian bowl, which cost £3 10s, and another, larger and gayer, but not so good.

Cairo
30.11.15

I'm in bed at the moment with what the doctor calls 'acclimatization', and Norman calls 'Gyppy Tummy'. The doctor seemed surprised I'd been out here all this time and hadn't had it before, and he gave me castor oil—the first time I've had it. And I'm living on milk, which is unpleasant, as it all has to be

55

boiled. It's the violent change in climate when the sun goes down which causes one's inside to go wrong.

Don't believe what you read in the Harmsworth press about the likelihood of Egypt being invaded. The Engineers and Artillery haven't been down on the Canal for a whole year doing nothing. They have made excellent roads on our side, and even some on the other. And it's said that the whole place is impregnable. Women and children are allowed to come out here by every boat, and lots of Australian women are here too. So don't feel alarmed.

The work at the hospital is very slack now, so it doesn't make much difference being away. The convalescent patients are being sent to Luxor and Cyprus, as well as to Alexandria and Port Said. The Yeomanry have left the Dardanelles and come to Mena House, and Norman's trying to locate his cousin Gilbert Solomon there. They went out 4,000 strong and came back only 800, mainly knocked out by dysentery and typhoid. They say the Turks have dysentery as badly as our men have.

Cairo
6.12.15

I have heard from the matron of the hospital that they are so empty now that there is nothing for me to do. It's the same everywhere; about 200 nurses are at the Semiramis Hotel, who have been told to occupy themselves getting up theatricals for Xmas, as they won't be needed till after then. By the way, if you hear of any officers' wives being sent away from Cairo, don't fash yourself. It's said that they occupy too much of their husbands' time, and talk too much. Mostly they are staying in hotels, which are supposed to be full of German agents too, and the officers' wives are often indiscreet and repeat things they have heard from their husbands. Civil servants' wives are in their own homes, and the Powers that Be are happy that they should stay.

I was sitting in the gardens at Gezirah one day with my Arabic grammar, when I saw the most homely sight in all Cairo—an elderly English nanny with a camp-stool and some sewing. We got talking; she said it was a heathenish country, because she had to say 'shy' instead of tea, and 'hellas' when she had finished. She'd never heard such nonsense!

I visited the hospital at the Citadel, and a friend took me all over it. It's very empty; the wards are huge palace halls, each with some hundred beds. As there were only a few men, they looked very dismal and lonely. There are large marble baths, which the RAMC use as store-rooms. I've also been to the Barrage, which is the place where the Nile starts branching into the Delta. There are fine gardens, with extensive views over the water. But, like everything else here, it's all artificial. How I long for something really natural. On another walk through the back streets of Cairo, we passed a boys' primary school and when we stopped to watch them drilling, the headmaster invited us in. It's a fine school; the fee is ten pounds a year, and he said that it only cost six thousand pounds for the five hundred and fifty boys. We saw them having their dinner—soup, meat and rice, and they behaved beautifully, using their utensils, including table-napkins, as well as any English boys would. Another day I walked alone to the Isle of Roda, the nearest approach to country in the neighbourhood, with maize fields and mud huts.

We went to the Synagogue for the Chanukah service for the soldiers. It was originally intended to be a Zionist meeting in the school, but the Governor of Cairo has just issued an order banning all political meetings, so that was knocked on the head. The service was good fun; it was timed to start at four, but when we got there a wedding was going on. The dresses were super-Mile End. The bride and bridegroom sat on high chairs by the Ark, facing the congregation, and a 'Talith' [prayer shawl] was used as a canopy. All their friends and relations talked the whole time the ceremony was going on. When it was over, our soldiers and officers lined up and gave them a guard of honour and military salutes, which much embarrassed the blushing, but very ugly, bride, but highly gratified the equally ugly bridesmaids. There were five officers, and the rest, men, nearly all Australians.

I went to fetch a young officer to take him a tour of the town—I'm becoming a good dragoman—from the Continental Hotel. The hotel is full of generals, and of foreigners, all sitting side by side in the lounge. It seemed odd, and not very good security. An abnormal number of generals are here now, and people seem to think it presages a big move. The Turks are

57

only eighty miles off from the Canal, but nobody seems to fear them much. Every night our troops on the Canal smooth down the sand, and look at it at dawn for footprints, in case any spies have got there and put mines in the Canal. There are all sorts of rumours about our attitude to Greece; if they are true, we don't seem to be very good at championing the cause of small nations.

I now spend some of my time at the Red Cross, tracing the wounded, and letting their relatives know about them. It's useful anyway, and I went to the Jewish school one day with Jack Mosseri. There are two ways of judging a school; either you think how good it is to have a school there at all, or else you criticize it as you would a school at home. By the first standard it's excellent; but by the second not so good, as the discipline is poor. They teach a lot of French, and hardly any English. They learn Italian because the Italian government sends out a teacher. I offered to go and teach some English, but Jack said their time-table was too full already, which was a good thing, as I don't think I'd be a very good teacher. Then I went on to tea with the Cattauis, who had a party for Australian officers. It was rather funny when I came to go. The old Pasha, very courteous and old-world, wanted to help me mount my bike, as if it had been a horse; he held it tightly, in case, I suppose, it should run away. Now one can't mount a bike when someone is holding it very tightly, and every time I tried to get on, I fell off. I was laughing so much, I couldn't think of the French to tell him not to hold it; and as he's a very fragile old man, I was afraid of hurting him. At last I blurted out: 'Il ne bouge pas comme ça', and he let go. Poor little man, I expect he was very stiff next day.

Jack's cousin took me for a drive in his car one day; he's the first man I've met who powders his face. Another day Norman and I went for a walk to Old Cairo, and when we stopped to look at a large building, a young man came out and asked us in. It was a bakery and steam mill, grinding corn for our army and millet for the Indian troops. The mixing of the dough for the bread has to be done in a dark room because of the flies. Next week we go to Alex to see the refugees from Palestine.

58

When the Turks declared war on the Allies, they announced that all residents of their Empire who were not Ottoman subjects must either become so at once, or leave the country. Of the Jews in Palestine, many had come from Eastern European countries. As foreigners they enjoyed certain privileges before the war, among them the great privilege of not being conscripted for national service. Many of them were reluctant to surrender these privileges, and ten thousand of them decided to leave the country. The American government, which was not then in the war, sent ships to evacuate those wanting to leave, and they were brought to Alexandria in the winter of 1914, and placed in camps. An English official of the Egyptian government, Mr Hornblower, a kindly and sympathetic man, was in charge of the camps. The expenses were paid by the English administration, with the help of money collected by committees formed in England and America; and a committee was formed in Egypt, to look after the welfare of the refugees. Norman was a member. There were, of course, a number of children among the refugees, and the redoubtable Miss Annie Landau, who had been headmistress of the Evelina de Rothschild Girls' school in Jerusalem for some years, took charge of an emergency school. We visited the camp, and I was impressed to hear the children sing 'God Save the King' and 'Home Sweet Home' in English, the latter, I thought, rather a tactless song to teach refugee children.

Norman attended a meeting of the Committee the day we went to Alex., and apparently the different factions among the refugees quarrel with each other as much in exile as they did in Palestine. I was asked to collect material in Cairo to make into clothes for the women and children, and on my return went with Jack Mosseri to the streets where the Jewish merchants who were in the trade had their warehouses, behind the Mousky, to beg them to give cloth and cotton for the refugees. We received whole pieces of cloth, some forty or fifty yards long, and we ended with over twelve hundred yards of material, collecting porters too as we went along, to carry the gifts. It was apparent how much more generous they were with their goods than with their money.

As I was continually writing in my letters home, Norman was not happy in his work at the Law School and longed to play a more active part in the war. But every effort he made to be released from the work there failed. A little before the New Year, however, one of his friends in the Government told him he was being released to join a new corps that was being formed, the Camel Transport Corps. The chief qualification needed was a knowledge of Arabic, which Norman had. So, never one to waste time, Norman wrote straight off to the Colonel of the new Corps, received a reply in two days, went to see him the next day, and was told he would be welcome in the Corps if he could be released. Here at last he was successful. The General in charge of the Cairo area had written to all the Ministries that officers were wanted for the Corps who must be able to talk Arabic, and that every available man must be spared. So there was no alternative but to let him go. It was easy for him to settle with other lecturers to take over his work; they readily consented, though till then he had been considered indispensable. An Indian tailor made his uniform in two days, and he took with him camping equipment which his sister had given us for a wedding present.

At first the Corps was to consist of twenty thousand camels and ten thousand fellaheen (Egyptian peasants) to look after them. Each four hundred camels and two hundred fellaheen was a section, with two British or Australian non-commissioned officers and one British subaltern. Over each five sections was a captain, and over the whole a colonel. The Corps' sole use was for transport, as the fellaheen were not drilled or allowed to have arms. At first they mainly transported ammunition, food and water from the railway head to the troops. It was pleasant for Norman that a number of his friends joined at the same time. It was more congenial than joining an ordinary regiment as a subaltern with boys who had just left school. He turned out to be a good rider, mainly on horseback, though at times he rode a fast riding-camel. The Egyptian government was prepared to lend him for the duration of the war, and pay his salary, as long as he undertook to return to the Law School. Later, as the Army neared Palestine, and he could see at last his dream of being able to work there coming true, he notified the authorities he would not be returning, and the pay stopped.

I did not write home about Norman joining the army until he was actually in camp in the desert to the east of Cairo. With two over-devoted families all those miles away, it seemed best to us to take our decisions, and avoid long-distance discussions and arguments. After all, Norman was by then thirty-two, and I was twenty-three; quite old enough to make up our own minds. I know my family were only too glad that his mind was more at ease—as I was. I decided to remain in Cairo so long as he was near enough to come home for the odd nights. I continue with extracts from the letters.

Cairo
10.1.16

I've at last been taken on again in a hospital; this time it's the Red Cross hospital at Giza. I catch a bus—i.e. a motor-ambulance—by the barracks at 7.45 every morning, and come back the same way at 1 pm. Over a thousand patients are in the hospital itself and the annexe, in which I work, when they are full, but they are still fairly empty. The annexe is in the Agricultural College, and the main hospital uses the building of a secondary school. It's not easy for a fairly recent comer like me to get taken on, as all those who worked so hard when the need was greatest want to work again. But I think they've taken me out of pity, as my husband has abandoned me so soon after we're married. I hear I'm alluded to at the Club as 'the poor little deserted bride'. They mean well.

There's a distinction here between VADs and probationers. There are no VADs in my annexe, only four sisters and four other pros, all of whom live in. For some reason the VADs aren't popular here. Apparently they are apt to give themselves airs. The pros with whom I work belong to the less 'social' British families, like railway officials. The matron, the very nice widow of a judge, and a trained nurse, found me getting friendly with them the first day, and asking one to tea on her day off. She drew me aside after, and told me these girls, though very nice, weren't my 'kind', and she thought she'd better warn me. That's life in Cairo! Anyway, I'm a registered Red Cross worker. Friday we got the order that all possible cases were to be removed to convalescent homes—I suppose all to do with what is happening at the Dardanelles. They are said to be evacuating Hellas, and want accommodation in case things go wrong. But apparently things didn't go wrong, and both nurses and men are grumbling at being so empty.

My 'sister' is a dear little Scotch woman, and the men like

her so much that they have given me two pounds to buy her a present in the Mousky. The only thing I get told off for is carrying things about myself, instead of clapping my hands for a native orderly to carry them. The Matron apologized to me because someone told me to wash down the doors, and she said I should never be doing a thing like that. She asked if I would mind helping mend the linen, but when she found me scratching my head, wondering which way a patch was put on, she tactfully suggested I should sort the clothes instead. Esther is to come and help with mending the linen instead of me. Rather humiliating!

Norman is very happy. He's under Major Blake, the head of the Cairo Fire Brigade, whom he likes very much, and is acting adjutant. The wife of another officer and I ventured to visit the camp one day, and there was Norman riding about on a lovely little Arab horse, looking as if he'd been at it all his life. The camp is an impressive sight; camels everywhere, lying down in their lines, standing up, or walking about in groups. We saw about five hundred arrive, with their attendants. The fellaheen are dressed in all sorts of colours, and each has a variegated blanket, to make them invisible in the desert. They get seven piastres a day—about one shilling and fivepence, which is more than the Tommies get; but all the same, there is a great deal of desertion. We walked round the acres and acres of camels, with a few tents for officers, and then had tea in one of the tents with a friend of Norman's—quite against the rules. When the Colonel galloped round, we hid under the beds, in case he saw us. But Norman blithely shouted out, as he rode past: 'Has anyone seen my wife?' But nothing happened. An aeroplane went overhead while we were there—how incongruous, aircraft and camels. Some evenings, Norman manages to slip away and spend a little time at home. And other evenings he telephones to me. One officer told me that the Camel Transport Corps is the best sport, the best training, the best view of the fighting, and no danger. It sounds good.

It has been bitterly cold some days, and we've had a bit of rain, very welcome after all that sunshine. No arrangement is made for rain here, and it comes into the houses. My bedroom was flooded one evening—and the streets are quite impassable after rain, as there are no gutters. We have a fire-place in one room, but coal is so expensive that, when I have a fire, I ask all my friends in from the rest of the house to come and share it. Other nights someone else has the fire, and I go and share. I still go down to the Guides some evenings a week. They are now getting their uniforms.

Cairo
18.1.16

There were only four men in our ward today, and all are up and walking about. But when we heard that the wife of the Resident was coming to visit us, we tucked a couple back into bed, to look more interesting.

I went out to dinner the other night, and before I went I was asked if I'd *mind* meeting an Egyptian! It's the first time I've met one at a party. He was rather amusing, but a bit oily in his manner: he is a Bey, and quite high up in the Public Works. We were talking of Socialism, and he said he was a Socialist, because he owned no property, but his mother wasn't because she did. A queer definition.

Cairo
3.2.16

I went to lunch with a friend one day, directly from the hospital, and there, to my surprise, was Norman—feeling very annoyed, as he'd been recalled from the Army to deal with Trading with the Enemy cases, which was work he'd been begging to be allowed to do ever since we came back, but was told he wasn't wanted for it. Anyway, he went to see Lord Edward Cecil at the Ministry of Finance, who was sympathetic, and told Norman that, if he could think of some way in which they could have the work done without taking him from the army, they'd be pleased to let him remain in the Camel Corps. So for hours on end Norman went here and there arranging things, and next day returned to camp a contented officer. The trouble was that an official senior to Norman who had been put on the job proved quite incapable of doing it. It was amusing: Norman had to see Lord Edward and Judge Kershaw the first afternoon, and they told him to come and meet them at the Sports Club. He found them just going to start a game of golf, and they said they couldn't see him till they'd finished. He returned later, and found them only at the 15th hole, and they refused to notice his existence till they'd finished the round. Meanwhile I went to the Police stores to buy him a revolver, quite sure that he'd win in the end. In the evening we were very extravagant and lit a fire, though coal is now £8 15s a ton, and oil unavailable for primuses, as it's held up at Alex and Port Said by the movement of troops.

I took the Girl Guides, with Esther to help, up to the Mokattam hills one afternoon. Hardly any of the girls had been there before, and three of their school-teachers asked if they could come too, as they'd never been either. And many of the girls had never been out to the Pyramids. While the girls were sitting there singing Hebrew songs, a group of native lads came and sat near, and clapped them when they'd finished, and then started singing Arabic songs to us. I get all the money I need for the Guides from the school committee: they're more generous than the LCC was in London.

At the Hospital yesterday, I was in charge of the ward, now with fifteen men, as the sister was ill. Sir John Rogers, the head of the Red Cross here, came round on a tour of inspection, but I managed all right.

I met an Australian out at tea, full of depressing stories about the blunders on the Peninsula, and saying unpleasant things about the British army. There is a great rivalry between the Australians and the British. The British—i.e. Esther's Military Policeman boy friend—say the Australians are continually murdered by the natives because they go prowling after their women, and five hundred Australians are unaccounted for.

Norman hasn't come in tonight, as I hoped he would. There's been trouble in his company. They changed the fellaheen for Egyptian army reserves, just in his company, and a day or so ago they all mutinied and went off. It's the fault of the British, they aren't being paid as much as the fellaheen, and they haven't been given all that's owed them. They went to try to petition the Sultan yesterday, and the Military Police (including Esther's young man) were called in to disperse them, and they had a bit of a scrap. But now it's all over, and six hundred of the reservists are in prison; and this means that

Norman's company won't move off eastwards with the rest, and will be in the present camp for another fortnight.

Norman has been in, and I've heard the rest of the story. All the reservists didn't go off together, and the remainder had planned to go yesterday. The Australians were called in to guard the camp, and they took these men prisoners, and flogged the ring-leaders. But it really is the fault of the Government. They still owe these men money from the time when they were conscripted into the army, and when these reservists went to get their pay, and asked for the back money, they were told they couldn't have it yet. So they walked off.

I went again one afternoon (before the trouble) to Norman's camp, to try and take photographs of the camels. But I didn't succeed. Camels are such terrifying beasts. If they get loose, they'll run straight at you. I got scared, and took refuge in a tent; but when I looked out, the same camels were waiting for me. And they can bite pretty badly; not a clean bite, like a dog, but a sort of chewing, and can take a man's arm off easily. It's happened in the camp. So I waited in the tent till Norman rode up, and sent someone to drive the camels away. Of course, I shouldn't be there, so again I ducked under the bed whenever a senior officer turned up. But it'll be the last time, I expect, as the company now has fellaheen from Assiut to replace the reservists, and will go off very soon.

Norman has gone off on active service, and is at the moment trekking in the desert east of here, with two Australian NCOs, two hundred fellaheen from Assiut, and four hundred camels. He goes to near Ismailia, and will probably get there tomorrow. That will be his base, and from there they will be sent off for a few days into the desert, and then return to the base. He took a box of provisions to supplement the bully beef and biscuits, which is all they get on trek.

Mesopotamia is very serious. People say we must reach Baghdad before the Russians, or else it will be bad for India.

There seems to be trouble brewing in India, and most of the Indian troops from here have been sent back. The Senussi business in the Western Desert isn't taken very seriously, and people don't seem to think the Xmas Day show was a great success. The Bucks Hussars got badly cut up; I hear they were caught in a trap. Norman's cousin Gilbert is out there in the Western Desert, and describes it as just a jolly seaside picnic. It's really not very important.

To get away from the war. I've had a tea-party of nine convalescent men from my ward. They were a mixed bag, including a South Wales miner, an Edmonton coster-monger, a Highland grocer, a Lancashire pot-boy, a Staffordshire baker, a Bucks policeman, a London coachman, a Manchester clerk, and a young snob from Wimbledon. An average mixture. There was not one word of war the whole afternoon, and never a mention of Egypt or Gallipoli, although they'd all seen plenty of active service. And, curiously, not a word about army life either. They just talked about 'Blighty', and their own particular corner of it. And it's always the same in the hospital. The party was a success. Various young women friends came in to help; we had an enormous tea, and played childish games, and they sang songs, and I think really enjoyed it. They didn't want to go when I had to take them back. And they behaved beautifully. The next morning, curiously, the men all got a touch of what they call 'Blighty Fever'. It was started by Jock, the Highlander, who started telling us about his home at the foot of the Loch, and some of the villagers talking only the 'Gaelic', and he talked of the Sabbath, when the Minister thought it a sin if he saw you going for a walk to enjoy yourself. And then the Lancashire boy started off about his mill-lassie, and then one whistled 'Little Grey Home in the West', and another 'Home Sweet Home', and then they all started getting cross and miserable, and I was feeling as cross and homesick as the rest. It just comes over you sometimes. Even the young snob was miserable. and refused to eat his dinner. Perhaps I like working in the hospital, because when I'm there I forget I'm in Egypt, like other British women try to do. Except for the native orderlies we might well be in London.

I was homesick all the time I was in Cairo; not for my

particular home, but for England, and especially London. I remember sitting on my balcony, tears streaming down my face, longing for the Tottenham Court Road on a wet February afternoon, and cursing the everlasting sunshine. I had plenty of extremely kind friends, who took a lot of trouble to see that I was never lonely. But I felt a fish out of water. I was at the stage, which of course I should have outgrown by the time I was twenty-four, when I felt that nobody appreciated my unconventional outlook on life, and I was beginning to think myself rather a superior sort of person. Reading my letters I wrote then, I find I actually say that. My mother would write back, chiding me for my conceit, and wondering why I was so full of complaints when I was having such an interesting and lively time. It was difficult to explain; but all the time I was in Cairo I seemed to be living on the surface of life, and never getting really into it.

I am amazed that the stories I tell about the war, and the movement of Norman's Camel Corps, ever passed the censor. Never once was a remark blacked out; and the same was true of the letters which Norman wrote me about the campaign in which he was engaged, after I had returned to England. There seems no explanation for this, other than that the letters were never read.

About this time I had a scare. One very hot evening I went to the stuffy cinema with a friend and two Australian officers. We sat in a box, and the officer sitting next to me complained that he was feeling ill, and probably had malaria. Next day his friend rang up to say that the officer who was feeling ill actually had smallpox (he eventually died), and hoped I had been vaccinated. I had not been since I was a young child, and when I went to the doctor and asked him to vaccinate me, he said it was too late to help in this particular case. I went through a few anxious days, not liking to tell anyone about it, but fortunately I did not catch it. A little later Norman wrote from the village of Salahiya, where he was stationed, to say there was an outbreak of smallpox, and all his camel-men had to be vaccinated. Normally it was done by making a cross incision with a razor-blade held in a pair of scissors, and putting in the vaccine. But the Moslem natives objected to a cross cut in their arms, so they had to be scratched with a scalpel, as I was.

My mother kept urging me to return to England, now that Norman was in the Army. But I refused to go as long as there were chances of the occasional leave. And at this time there were such chances. One evening he arrived at 8.30. The General of the 15th Division, to which he was attached, had received a cable from Cairo to say that Lieut. Bentwich of the CTC was to proceed to Alex at once to give secret information to Mr R., and they were to ascertain if the above officer understood the nature of the mission and the allusion. Norman had already been in correspondence with a man in the Intelligence, so he understood the allusion. He carefully missed the train which would have connected with Alex, and came home for the night, and left early in the morning, quite excited about his secret mission.

Some months later he had to vouch for the authenticity of Aaron Aaronson, whom he knew well. Aaronson was a well-known agriculturist from Zichron-Jacob, the village in Palestine where, before the war, Norman's sister and her husband had settled. Aaronson had a plan to run an intelligence organization in Palestine to help the British. Later they were known as the Nili spies, about whom much has been written in recent years. By signalling to British ships out at sea from the village, which is on a spur of Mount Carmel, and by using carrier pigeons, and occasionally infiltrating through the Turkish lines, these young men and women did valuable work, until they were caught. Aaronson's sister was so tortured that she committed suicide.

Cairo Intelligence wanted to be quite sure of his good faith, and this was where Norman came in. His intelligence work also brought Norman in contact with T.E.Lawrence—Lawrence of Arabia—whom he already knew from before the war. He came to Cairo unexpectedly for intelligence work on other occasions, and was useful because of his knowledge of the Zionists and Palestine. It was impressive to have dispatch riders, with blue bands round their arms coming and going around our flat, and all letters had 'By Safe Hand' written on them. He told me on one occasion that the British were not going to invade Palestine yet, because the French were not ready, and were not prepared for Britain to do it on its own. They wanted to lay claim to parts of Palestine and Syria after the war.

Sometimes on these mysterious visits he had leave to stay longer, and we enjoyed trips on the Nile in a felucca (a sailing boat), or moonlight walks on the Mokattam hills, or evening picnics at the Pyramids. I enjoyed the Pyramids more by night than by day—I was able to forget the misery of the poor devils who had died building them, when I saw them in the dim light. And the Sphinx looked less like a picture postcard.

On one occasion Norman told me that he had seen transports of Russians going through the Canal; he had seen them himself, not like the hearsay of the Russians with snow on their boots in England at the beginning of the war. He was not sure if they came from the Persian Gulf, or all the way round from Siberia. The Cairo rumour at this time was that there was to be a joint landing at Alexandretta, on the Syrian coast, by British, French and Russian troops.

On another occasion he came in to buy equipment for his mess, and managed to miss the train back. And another time he appeared with an NCO to collect money. He was still only a Second Lieutenant. One of his friends told me that the Adjutant had said they could not think of a rank compatible with his genius on most subjects and his ignorance of military subjects in particular. However, later he received promotion, and when he left the Camel Corps in 1918, it was with the rank of a Major.

I continue with my letters, which in March were still mainly about my work in the hospital:

One day everything in the hospital was scrubbed and washed down, and we were given clean covers and mosquito curtains, and little blue bows to tie them back. And pots of marigolds and cineraria and other flowers suddenly appeared. All because the Sultan was paying a visit to the hospital. He went first to the main building, and they telephoned through that he was on his way to our Annexe, so we lined up in the hall, with clean aprons and armbands. When the cars drove up, out got Sir John Maxwell, the GOC, and Sir John Rogers, the head of the Red Cross, and some Battenberg Prince, but no Sultan. He'd got bored, and gone home, and everyone was annoyed with him. The men were disappointed, and so were the orderlies, who'd been issued with new *galabiehs* [white robes] and new socks, for the occasion. It was rotten of him; he'd done exactly the same last year when he visited the Law School, and missed Norman's class, as it was upstairs. Maxwell was very nice, and talked to every man for a few minutes. His train of titled popinjays looked more like caricatures out of a German newspaper than real officers. There are far too many brass hats here, and they seem to spend too much time frivolling. It's said there were 107 generals here at one time.

I've discovered something about the men. I was commenting to two of them what a shame it was that so many young men had got bad hearts making them unfit for active service—it's generally known as 'Blighty Heart', as they have to be sent home. These men said, if I wouldn't 'tell on them', they'd explain why. It seems they chew cordite and take salt pills, and the effect is to upset their hearts. They said that the doctors on the Peninsular saw through the trick, and so do those in France; but in Egypt they don't yet see through it. It's so mad, because apparently they'll have these bad hearts for the rest of their lives. But some of them will do anything to be out of the war here—though most of them are anxious to fight again, somewhere else. It's just two of my particular lads who have been up to this trick.

Cairo
14.3.16

The oppressive Khamseen [hot wind] is on us again, and frequent sand-storms, like London fogs. This weather brings out the insects, and the favourite sport in my ward at present is flea-hunting. In our flat I think nothing of catching them in the sitting-room, and one even talks about them when paying calls. They are part of life here. 'My' boys broke bounds the other night, and found their way to a native village, and started kissing the women. So they're in disgrace, and as they are all really fit to leave, and the rest of the wards are as empty too, the Annexe is being closed, and I'm going over to the main building. I'm really dispensable, but I've nothing else to do if I don't go to the hospital; so I begged to be allowed to stay on.

There's a fantastic rumour that a large party of British VADS arrived here, and were told they weren't needed, but at Mespot. they were crying out for them. However, Mespot. is under the India Office and here, I suppose, we are under the Foreign Office. So they had to go all the way home and start again. You may believe these rumours or not, as you like.

Be prepared for a shock. I'm now an employee of the Ministry of Finance, in the capacity of a clerk and typist, at the princely sum of £14 a month, signed on for one month at a time, with the right of either side to give a month's notice. I've taken it on for one month to start with. It's an innovation employing women clerks in the Egyptian government; till now they've had four. I heard through a friend that one was going home, so I wrote to Mr Ward-Boys, one of the chief people there. I went to be interviewed by him and some other men, and was sat down at a typewriter, which fortunately was a French one, so I said I couldn't manage it without practice. It's all bluff, because, as you know, I only type with one finger. But there's a lot of filing, at which I'm quite practised. The main thing, however, is it's terribly confidential, and they seem to think the wife of a senior offical has that qualification. At any rate, I heard nothing for a fortnight, but yesterday I had a letter from Goschen himself, one of the top people, saying they'd take me on. So this morning I went there, and said I'd come to start at once, which rather surprised him, because they aren't used to such hustle in the Government here. Goschen said he was only able to pay me £14 a month, as I was to be temporary. But this is almost the same as Norman's pay, except that he has free lodging.

I work in an airy little office with (she says under) a much older woman who is a professional secretary from England. I think those who engaged me, who know Norman well, believe that I've got into debt, and am using this as a way out. Other wives don't ask for typists' jobs. The hours are from 9 to 1.30, and no work on Fridays, the national day of rest. I didn't feel I was behaving badly to the hospital, because they'd so little work for us. They had to put another girl on to help me, to find her something to do; and it became a competition which of us could get there in time to wash the men first.

The news this week is bad; a disaster on the Canal. Norman, who is at Kantara, was out of the fight, but some of the other camel companies were in it. Apparently our troops advanced eastwards without any outposts or aeroplane cover, and they took a Turkish outpost, at the same time as the Turks with the help of Germans moved westwards, on a more northern route, and came to our outpost at Katia. They surprised the Worcesters, who were still in their pyjamas, and had no machine guns, but only rifles, and two squadrons were simply wiped out. And any amount of stores, as well as military information, was captured by the enemy. General Murray apparently wanted it kept quiet, and was furious when the facts leaked out. Everything is depressing, because, on top of that, Kut has fallen in Mespot., and there's the rebellion in Ireland. Norman wrote me one pleasant feature; the Turks put bread and water by the side of the wounded they couldn't take away. Different from the Germans. The Tommies say, 'Johnny Abdul is a clean fighter.'

Cairo
16.5.16

It's queer. In the English papers you had an account of the scrap on the Canal—albeit a very false one—two days before anything was known about it here. It makes one realize that things must be a good deal worse than we are told.

Jack Mosseri and the Jewish community keep pestering me to go on the Ladies sub-committee of this and that. And I tell them I'm like my mother, and refuse to go on a ladies sub-committee just because I'm a woman. I said I'd be prepared to go on the main committee, and help them run their schools and clinics, but Cattaui Pasha, who is the big noise, wouldn't hear of that, so I just keep to my Girl Guides, and that's all I do for the Jewish community. There are 1,500 boys and girls in the schools, and no women on the committee running them. The girls learn sewing every day, and when I asked if they learned cooking, he said, of course not, they weren't going to be cooks. I suppose they want them all to be dressmakers.

Cairo
25.5.16

We're frightfully busy in our office, and it's good to feel that I'm really doing something useful, after the last slack weeks at the hospital. It's interesting work, in connection with Enemy Trading and Granting Licences, and that's all I can safely tell

72

you. The woman whose room I share talks too much when I want to get on with the work, telling me all her dull family history—but although she's 'Mrs' never a word about a husband.

Gilbert Solomon has been staying with me on leave, and it shocks the British respectable people opposite when they see us having breakfast together on the balcony. One evening we took the tram to Heliopolis, and rode on donkeys up the Suez road across the desert, and picnicked by the second watchtower. It was a full moon. Before the Suez Canal was made, passengers going to India landed on the Egyptian coast, rode over the desert to Suez, and then embarked on another ship. Friday we went to the Barrage by train. He, as a private, is only supposed to travel third class. I, as the wife of a senior official, am expected to travel first. In the end, we both went first and hoped a military policeman wouldn't spot him.

Cairo
10.6.16

Today, while Helen Bailey and I were playing golf at the Club, the news was spread around about Kitchener being drowned. The first reaction at the Club was to laugh it away, as a Cairo rumour, but when it was said to be true, people were absolutely stunned. He was so known here. It's bad for our prestige for the natives to know that we can't even look after a man like him properly. Whether they liked him or not I don't know, but they thought him the most important of all Englishmen. It's ghastly to think how pleased the Germans will be.

Norman was now moving further and further away from Cairo, and was unable to come home for the odd nights. Cairo had become unusually hot, with a temperature of 117 degrees in the shade. My hands would be badly scorched if I touched the steel on my bicycle when I left the Ministry to ride back for lunch. So I decided to return to England, believing in a muddled way, that I would return again in the autumn, as wives did in peacetime. I handed in my notice at the Ministry who soon found someone more professional for the work, and sailed from Port Said on the *Caledonia*, the ship on which we had travelled in the autumn.

Esther was with me, sad at leaving her military policeman, to whom she was now officially engaged. Fortunately for me, Miss Bailey was on the same ship, and we shared a cabin. She was the most delightful of travelling companions. Port-holes had to be shut, because of fear of submarines; so we took our bedding up on deck. When the crew woke us, soon after dawn, to wash down the deck, we planned to finish our sleep in the cabin below. But the first morning I attempted to do this, an enormous black rat was on my bed. Except for this incident, we had a comfortable and safe journey to Marseilles. One night we stopped in the pitch dark for six hours, because the captain had heard there was a submarine around, looking for a French transport. It's queer how uncanny it seems when the ship stops in mid-ocean, and all is deathly quiet. We arrived at Marseilles; and because my uncle Herbert Samuel had asked that we should be sure to find a place on the P & O special although we were travelling second class, we had an easy journey back to London.

1916—1917

Woolwich Arsenal

My family was not really used to having its members living abroad, so when I arrived home I received a tremendous welcome, in which Norman's family joined. I was naturally anxious to note the changes there had been in England during my absence. And the first that struck me was the national emphasis on 'economy'. Shortages were being felt because of the submarines, and to be sparing of everything, to be what we used to call 'stingy', was the order of the day. My first morning home I accompanied my mother, who was active in the economy campaign, to a National Economy Exhibition at Prince's Ice Rink, at which royalty appeared. There seemed to me somewhat an air of patronage about it all; the old tradition of the 'ladies' exhorting the 'women'. Many, like my mother, set them a good example, but not all. She told me of a woman she had heard say: 'I really can't be expected to go without the two meat meals a day I have always been used to. And I couldn't expect to keep my butler and the other servants if I cut down on their meals. So really, I don't see how I can economize.' Economy was still one of the 'good works', and not yet a national necessity.

I went next day with a friend who was helping the campaign in Bethnal Green, distributing pamphlets from house to house. I never knew that area before, although it is a near neighbour of my favourite Stepney. It seemed dingier and more squalid than Whitechapel, but that may have been because I had no chance to explore its alleys and byways, always the most interesting parts. We had also to urge people to buy War Loans as a form of patriotism. It seemed to be a queer form, because we had to tell them that for every 15s 6d they lent the country now, they would receive a pound later on. Almost invariably, they would answer 'We prefer the Post Office Savings', and when we tried to explain that this was not such an advantage to them, they gave the invariable answer 'I'm very grateful, I'm sure, but not today, thank you.' It was nice to be back among the dear, delightful Cockneys.

But for all this I felt flat and disillusioned. I'd been glamourizing England so much while I was in Cairo—even the Tottenham Court Road—and now I'd come back to it, all the glamour had gone. I was at a loose end, and out of everything. People were so busy, and although I could lend a hand here and there for the odd day, I did not yet 'belong' to the 'war workers'. I started with the plan to have a holiday in England, during the Cairo summer, and then return there. I knew I could find another confidential job in one of the Ministries, so I went to Pitmans and enrolled to learn shorthand and professional typing.

It was a curious place, unlike anything I had experienced before. Rows and rows, mainly of girls, utterly purposeful, which, regretfully, I was not. I was not sufficiently sure it was what I wanted to do. I should have had to give much more concentrated attention to it than I seemed capable of doing at that time, if I were to master the skill. So all too soon I abandoned the effort.

I went to the Old Paulinas' annual meeting at the school, wondering what my contemporaries were doing, and hoping to find out from my old friends what possibilities of useful work there were if I remained in England. Many of them were teaching; a few were married, and starting families; and those actively engaged in war work were mainly nursing. One or two were definitely opposed to the war, and on the fringe of pacifist organizations. But I felt no more drawn to pacifism than I had been at the beginning of the war. Most of the afternoon I spent talking in the swimming bath, remembering the heat in Cairo. How often had I sat in Cairo remembering the lovely coolness of the school swimming bath!

Miss Gray, with that rare knack of being equally interested in every old girl, whether she were a success or a nonentity, talked to me for some time. I was sorry to find I had missed meeting other Old Paulinas who were in Cairo at the same time as I was, and she said she would act on a suggestion of mine, which was that any old girls should be asked through the school magazine to tell her when they were going abroad. If any two or more were in the same place, she would let them know that the others were there too.

I spent some time with the Whitechapel Guides, and I made arrangements for them to camp again at Chartridge in August. They were pleased to see me, but tongue-tied and unemotional as girls of that age were, in that generation. 'Hullo, you all right', was the general greeting, and then we behaved as if I had never been away. Most were now at work, mainly tailoring, making uniforms. One or two were at secondary schools, one holding to her intention of becoming a doctor. The non-Jewish girls in the company, of which there were only one or two, were helping their parents in the street market. There was much talk in the East End about the order which the Government had made declaring that all non-naturalized aliens must either join the Forces, or return to their country of origin. The enemy aliens were, of course, interned. Many of the young men would have liked to join the Forces before this, but were not accepted, and so they had continued with their civilian work, often earning very high wages and walking about dressed in the height of fashion, and arousing considerable resentment.

Herbert Samuel, now the Home Secretary, wanted to hear all I could tell him about conditions and affairs in Egypt, and I breakfasted with him one morning. I found it an embarrassing interview, as I was uncertain whether he wanted my personal view, or just factual information, which anyway he could always obtain from many other sources. So I was conceited enough to give him my own opinions about life and events there. He came to stay with us for a few days at Chartridge, and while there a fire broke out locally, to which he, and all the household, went, to see if they could be of use. He was annoyed later to see a paragraph in the papers mentioning his attempts to help at the fire, and adding that he had afterwards distributed beer and cigarettes to the firemen. As Home Secretary he was, I presume, responsible for the 'no treating' order; and he had given up both drinking and smoking for the duration of the war. He issued an official denial of the story.

At the end of July, news came that the local battalion of the Bucks and Oxford Light Infantry had been badly cut up in France, and scarcely a family in Chartridge and the surrounding villages was without some member killed or wounded. I think this shocked me into a fuller realization of the war than anything else that happened at that time; all the boys, from the farms, the cottages, and the squire's houses, with whom we'd played cricket in the summer holidays, struck down in one day. I pulled myself together, and decided I'd had enough of this 'being on leave' life, going to parties and theatres, playing tennis and endlessly talking. I was committed to the Girl Guide camp in August, and had promised to spend a fortnight with Alice and some friends on the river near Oxford afterwards. I wrote to Norman to say that I had finally decided not to return to Egypt, but to find some serious war work in England. But it was not till 3 September, two months after my return home, that I finally found the work I wanted to do. I am rather ashamed of those two months of pleasure and laziness.

My brother Hugh, who was working in the office at Woolwich Arsenal, suggested that, with my experience of social work, I should apply for a post there, as a Welfare Superior. Here are extracts from the letters I wrote to Norman, after this:

London
7.9.16

Our first wedding anniversary, but I don't feel excited. Wedding days without husbands are really rather flat. But it was nice to get your cable; and good of you to say you didn't mind my staying on here to do a job. I've actually got one, as a Principal Overlooker at Woolwich Arsenal, with the princely wages of £4 10s a week, working from 7 am till 7 pm for six days, and then from 7 pm till 7 am for seven nights. I know the hours are terribly long, but if other girls can stand them, why shouldn't I? Your family were shocked when I told them about it, and quite disapproving at my getting a factory job. Fortunately, my family seem glad I've settled on something. While I'm about it I might as well do a real piece of war work as play at it, as I've really done up till now.

It really is a good job I've got, high in the factory hierarchy, and I hope to work my way up later on to a staff job. Hugh wanted me to be a 'lady supervisor', which would have meant looking after the general welfare and conduct of the women and girls in the factory. It's a staff job, working only in the day-time, and not such long hours, and paid by the month, and not by the week though, curiously, with less money. I applied for this job to Miss Lilian Barker, chief 'lady superintendent', a short-haired, very capable, unconventional sort of middle-aged woman. She asked me about all I'd done before, but as I'd no previous experience of factory life, she thought I'd better go into the factory as an overlooker first, and if at Christmas I still wanted to be a supervisor, I could apply again. It's best to get to know the girls first, before I try to 'supervise' them. So she sent me to see the Manager, and he asked me a lot of questions, and suddenly said 'Are you frightened of figures?' I said I was fairly at home with ordinary sums. 'Can you do decimals?' he asked. I said yes. Then he wanted to know if I'd ever used a slide-rule, and again I said yes. Then he asked if I thought I could supervise twenty men and women who were analysing textiles, and see that their calculations and deductions were correct. He showed me sample figures, mainly percentages, and I told him I could easily manage them; and he also asked about simple physics analyses, which I told him I'd done at College. He said that the twenty people I'd be looking after were overlookers, and that they in their turn were responsible for the work done by the people in the Tailor's Shop, and did I think I could take it on? I said, what did *he* think; after all, it was he who was engaging me. So we sat for some time, looking at each other, each waiting for the other to answer. At last he said I could try, because, if I could do the figures and the calculations, the rest should be fairly easy. I thanked him, and he engaged me on the spot. I'm lucky, because Principal Overlookers *ought* to have been trained as Overlookers, and I suppose I should have more knowledge than I have of maths.

His secretary ran after me as I left, and said she was *so* glad I'd got it, as it had been run by men before and had been such a muddle, and she knew I could manage it, and she also said how much better women did things than men. She added *she'd* have got the job if she'd been any good at figures, but she wasn't.

Hugh is second-in-command of the pay department, with a hundred and thirty clerks under him. It's an important position here. I went back to Miss Barker to sign on, and I put as my references Uncle Herbert and my cousin Edwin Montagu; the Home Secretary and the Minister of Munitions should really be good enough. Hugh suggested I gave their names, though I thought it a bit showing-off. Then I had to be examined by the Doctor, which was an unpleasant process. A number of women cleaners were being examined at the same time, and we all had to undress together, and stand there naked, waiting for the doctor. I had to keep reminding myself I was a Socialist, and mustn't mind. Heart, nerves, veins in the legs and eyes were what she looked at, and heads (for lice). When she came to me, she said: 'You oughtn't to be among this lot. Aren't you a public-school girl?' And me a Socialist! Of course, I passed easily, and then went along to Hugh, where the final signing-on had to be done, under his supervision. I signed various compensation and unemployment and insurance forms, which they did not give me time to read. It's funny, the rate of pay is a very different thing from the pay I get. It's written on my paper as 25s a week. The rest is made up of overtime, night-work, and depends on the piece-rate in the factory to which I'm attached, the tailor's shop. It's far too complicated for me to understand. I have a conscience at getting such a good job without any qualifications, just through Hugh's influence. Apparently, it's the way things are done here. It's a pity I can't get a job on my own merits, but I just haven't any!

I'll live at home, at Porchester Terrace, but it means I'll have to get up very early in the morning. The only possible alternative is a Girls' Friendly Society Hostel near the Arsenal, which I'd hate. And on my Sundays off, I'll still be able to look after the Guides. (We are now meeting at Toynbee Hall.)

The police now carry out raids on men not in uniform, asking to see their papers. They raided Golders Green station the other night, near where Hugh lives, and took away some two hundred men. I was going home with Hugh, and saw them all being marched off, respectable-looking city types. Hugh was just too late for the raid—fortunately.

I'm feeling very patriotic. I turned out of a comfortable bed at
5 am this morning and wandered through pitch-dark, anti-
Zeppelin streets to the underground station, and got a ridicu-
lously cheap return ticket—7d—to Plumstead and back. I
decided to start in at once, because I remember you told me in
Cairo, when I got the job at the Ministry of Finance, always to
be ready to start a new job at once, and never pretend you had
anything more important to do. At Charing Cross the guard put
the girls in the first-class carriages, to keep them away from
the 'toughs'. I enjoyed seeing the dawn break, but I suppose
even that will pall after a time. I was pleased to find I could
buy *The Times* that early. When the guard had locked me in
alone in a first-class carriage, a crowd of men stormed the
carriage at the next station. One had a key, and unlocked the
door, saying to me: 'You can't expect a carriage to yerself
these days. We're all workers, and 'ave to get to work, so
we're coming in', and they came. But at the next station one of
them said: 'Better lock that door again, Bill. We don't want
'eaps of them crowding in 'ere.' Socialism is such a good
thing—for other people!

Coming into the Arsenal at 7 am is like going into a huge
fair. Crowds of people, mainly women, jostling and pushing,
half coming off night-work and the rest going on day-shift,
mixed up with strings of WD lorries, and trains careering
madly and importantly, seemingly going wherever they like.
And outside the Arsenal gates ice-cream, milk and cheap sweet
vendors galore. The queer thing is, everybody seems quite
silent, except for a certain amount of cheap humour and
curious love-making between men and girls. To be snobbish, I
suppose it's not necessarily the highest type of human who
comes as a cleaner, or even a factory hand, in the Arsenal.

In the tailor's shop the things made from textiles are
manufactured, and in the test room, where I'm the Principal
Overlooker, we test samples of these materials. I've ten men
and ten girls under me—here every female, even a grand-
mother, is a 'girl'—and two boys about 13. They are a friendly
community, all first names to each other (except me), and it's a
quiet place to work in, a partitioned-off corner of the large

factory, and the boss's office raised up in one corner, with glass all round, so that he sees us as well as the factory. To begin with, I have to go through all the testing processes myself—mainly tension machines, counting threads, testing for water-proofing, etc. I'm writing this in the lunch break. I've come out to have my lunch in a shop by the station, as I've not been able to find out about a canteen (nobody tells you anything!). The other girls bring lunch with them, and I'll do the same in future.

London
12.9.16

At the moment I'm sitting on a very hard stool, writing to you in the dinner hour, having eaten what I brought with me. The girls are all lying on piles of material we are testing, on the floor, or under the table. But I'm not yet sure if it's dignified for a PO to do that. But I'll really have to—this stool is terribly hard, twelve hours at a stretch! One of the men is called Reggie; he's very good-looking with curly hair. He is teaching me all about the machines. The alarm clock didn't alarm me this morning, and I didn't wake till ten minutes before the train left the station. I hadn't time for breakfast, but I took my bread and butter and cold fried fish and ate it in the train, with sixteen other people in the carriage. I'm already learning to live the 'Woolwich' way. As it's my job to report any of my room who are late, I can't very well be late too. I've learnt to analyse silk and felt and braid, and to use all the machines. and the others are very impressed with my knowledge of logarithms. And they're already telling me their life's history and ambitions, which after only one and a half days, shows me I'm 'accepted'.

The factory 'boss' interviewed me last night, and impressed on me the necessity for being accurate and checking everything. We are known as part of the 'Royal Laboratories', and everything used in any of the munition factories in England in the way of textiles, paper and leather has to be tested at Woolwich—and we do the textiles. Apparently I'm between Scylla and Charybdis, because, if I let a sub-standard material pass, there'll be dud shells and internal explosions inside shells, and gunners killed and other horrors; and if I turn down material as sub-standard without good cause, the contractors can take it up with the Chamber of Commerce, and if we *are* wrong—but here the boss explained that we never *had* been wrong, and that was the reputation I must keep up. Now it's time to start work again. We have a tank for testing with permanently boiling water, used for tea or cocoa. Tins of material for testing stand in it, to see what effect heat has on the stuff. The tins are greasy and dirty, but I imagine the boiling water kills the germs. Reggie, who is 20, gave me his photo today. But he rather spoilt any sentiment there might be by adding: 'I shouldn't talk to you in such a familiar way. You're probably old enough to be my mother!' He's 20 and I'm 24. I expect it's getting up so early is ageing me. He's the foreman of the room. But I am finding my feet, and am now in charge properly, and getting on fine.

London
15.9.16

I've succumbed, and am now lying on the floor in the dinner-hour, writing this. I couldn't stand any more of the backless stool. Reggie's going to make me a cushion for it. This group hasn't had anyone looking after them properly before, and they are frightfully slack. They take half an hour to settle down after every break, and knock off half an hour too early in the evening. And they make endless cups of tea, and gossip either about football and cars, or clothes and theatres (according to their sex) all the time. Some of them have no real interest in their work. One, I think, is hopeless, and she ought to go. When I told Reggie, he said 'Of course, she's married, and that makes 'em so blooming independent, there's no doing anything with 'em!' He's almost as bad as the rest, but is so unhappy if I criticize him, it's difficult. I find that all those over 21 get the same money as I do, so I think they ought to have a bit more conscience. I spend a lot of time checking their calculations, and I don't make *too* many mistakes.

We might almost be on the battlefield here. Great guns go off all the time, and the whole place shakes. But in the dinner hour I suffer more from the so-called singing of the factory next door than from the guns. There are a number of Arsenal songs and parodies, and they're not very tuneful! I'm picking up, and find myself using, the kind of expressions I thought only existed on the stage: 'I beg yours, if you apologise.' 'And then we woke up', if anyone tells a tall story. Any man is a 'John Willie', and the 'sorrow' they say instead of sorry is very catching.

I've had a letter from your father suggesting I should leave this and take some Zionist propaganda job. I've written back I prefer to be here.

London
28.9.16

I'm on night-shift. Theoretically, it's better than day, as the 'boss' isn't there hanging around and watching us from his glass cage, and I feel freer. There's plenty of work, and we are only eight girls and four men and one boy. We can sleep on the floor in the breaks. We have dinner-break from 11-12, and the shift after that is the worst, as we all get very sleepy. At 4.30, a half-hour break, and then on till 7. At times, I feel

> 'a mere machine of iron and wood
> That toils for Mammon's sake
> Without a brain to ponder and craze . . .'

I'm exaggerating, and really I'm enjoying it very much, sleepiness and all, and I find sums and card-indexing are now second nature. Of course, it's different for me from what it is for the others. I go home to a lovely bed, hot meals, and people looking after me. Some of the girls live on their own, and in the factory many are married with children. I think they're wonderful, the way they manage.

Whenever Zepps fly over the coast, we shut down, because all our buildings have glass roofs. But don't worry—it's very safe, as there are plenty of anti-aircraft guns to drive them off, and they've never yet done any harm at the Arsenal. I've not yet seen a Zepp, and all the room here is concerned about this, and promised to find me a good place to look from next time one is visible. Last night at 8.30 we were told Zepps were on their way, 9.30 we had to 'stand by', and at 1.40 lights went out. I was amazed at the quiet way in which the 1,000 girls in the factory took it. Those who wanted to go outside just fetched their hats and coats and went, and the others stayed and sang. Except for one young widow who had left her child alone at home. In cases like that, they are allowed to go home, and off she went. My group all stayed in. I encouraged them to do that, as I'm told there's too much larking among men and girls in the dark outside, and anyway there's a danger from shrapnel. After joining in the singing for a while, and hearing a noise like a train with a pain inside overhead, and being told there was nothing to see, we went back to our room and slept on the floor till 3.40, when the lights went on again, and we resumed work. Thus ended my first raid, very tame indeed.

The men make beds for the girls (including me) of hanks of braid covered with cambric, and when we lie down in the dinner hour at night they cover us with their coats, and usually themselves wash in the sink, and shave. It's all very decorous, and as well behaved as Gezira, if not better. There's a free and easy atmosphere, and the men are always ready to do the heavy work for the girls, and the girls supply the men with cups of tea. But it's not like that with the crowds in the street, and on the trains. Lots of them are very rough, and the language is amazing. One of my girls was a lady's maid, and has travelled in Italy and the Riviera. Some of the others are daughters of soldiers, and have lived in Egypt and India. The PO for the alternate shift is about fifty, and I should think a High School teacher in peacetime. She's new, too. The first night on duty I went to sleep at the 4.30 break, and never woke till 5.30. I found all the other girls asleep too, and Reggie and the rest of the men sitting on the table watching us—'keeping crow to see we weren't copped', as they put it. Nice of them, but bad for discipline. But we seem to get through the work somehow.

London
2.10.16

I'm feeling rather mean. A man under me is a Russian, and I happened to tell Hugh. Aliens aren't allowed to work in the Arsenal. He has a very foreign accent, and is a very unpleasant person. Today the boss sent for him, and I feel mean and nasty, though I don't suppose he'll guess I'm the cause. The other day the boss blamed the girls for making a mistake, so I went up and said I thought the mistake was due to the machine.

He replied: 'When you're as old as I am, you'll understand that machines are much less likely to make mistakes than human beings. So go along, and pitch into those girls all you know how.' I don't really know how to pitch into people, because I've such a fellow-feeling for people who make mistakes.

London
9.10.16

It's nearly midnight, and I'm lying on the floor writing this. I've now found that the room is extremely dirty—one shift comes on as the other goes off, so there's no time to clean it. It's also full of mice, which I hate. They run over us while we sleep, and we have to shoo them off our plates like flies while we eat. It's not as wonderful here as I thought.

I've succumbed again, and I'm finishing this during the shift. But there's not enough work this week for me, and if I did the girls' work, they wouldn't like it. It's having two POs. The day one does all the work, and leaves little for the night one to do. Some time I must explain this to the boss. He seems to be a sympathetic person. I had to sack a girl on Sunday night, and I hated it. She cried and said 'I'm so happy here, please let me stay.' But she's an inefficient little slacker, so I took her up to the boss, and he's found her a job in the factory at the same rate of pay. The other PO reached the limit the other day when she gave me orders about my work in a real school-marmish way. But I put her in her place and now she's quite humble. I've found out she's forty-one from Hugh, who has all the records, but we are supposed to be equals, and I resent her always trying to boss me. Reggie has just announced that 'a bloomin' animal with umpteen legs has come out of a pile of braid and walked across the table, and didn't half make him feel squiffy inside.' He poured gin on it to kill it. These huge bales of materials on a floor which is never cleaned harbour all kinds of beasts. But nobody gets ill, or seems any the worse.

London
15.10.16

I've now done five weeks at Woolwich, and haven't yet got the sack. I like my job immensely, so don't think I'm unhappy here because of some of the things I'm going to write about in this letter . . . These things, ugly as they are, don't usually affect me in the same way as they do the poor devils in the shops and at the machines, who can't just leave and go to any place where they are worked less hard, or are under better conditions, because of the Defence of the Realm Act. They wouldn't be able to get another job for some weeks. Some of them are worked so hard that they literally drop at their machines.

Something that happened on Wednesday night brought it home to me more than anything else what a hell life is for some here. It was an awfully hot and muggy night, and the factory to which we are attached, the tailor's shop, was simply fugged up with bad air. It never gets ventilated, as one shift has to be on before the other shift is off, and even day-time Sundays some hundreds of men are working there. You can imagine what it's like on an airless night. Many of the men who work in the factory are cobblers—snobbies, they call them—making shoes for use in the danger buildings. One of these men, an elderly fellow, collapsed by his machine, and his comrades carried him out. It was the third occasion he'd collapsed, and nobody seemed to bother about him. This caused a commotion among the thousand or so girls, and some of them fainted. And then in the dinner-hour one of the poor devils went outside with his sharp knife, and first cut open his hand and arm, then cut his throat open for five inches. And he wasn't found till the tea-break, at 4.30 am. He was still alive when one of the men in the factory found him. There is no foreman or forewoman in charge at night on that shift. The young man meant well, but he went round the girls asking if any of them knew first aid. They thought it was just a small accident, or someone fainting, and those who said they could went out, and when they saw all the blood and the cut throat just fainted. However, he was bound up somehow, although there was no proper first-aid outfit in the factory, as there should have been. They found a stretcher and carried him to the railway line that runs just outside, and telephoned for an ambulance, and had to wait half an hour before a railway engine could be found to bring it up. Reggie was called to take a hand with the ambulance, and returned filled with indignation at the delay, and the lack of

87

anyone in charge. By then, the girls in the factory were demoralized, and talking in groups with white faces and shaking knees. But the most awful confession is that I never went into the factory and attempted to take control. I felt as bad about it as anyone, and there seemed nothing I could do, as most of the girls were older than I was, and didn't know me. But I'm not proud of myself. Even at five in the morning I ought to show a bit more spirit of leadership. But when we left in the morning, and I saw the 'test room young ladies' jostling with the rest to gape at the blood still on the ground, I relieved my feelings by telling them what I thought of them. Of course it's ridiculous to write to you all this when hundreds are dying in battle every day. But the callous way authority treats the workers gets me down.

I was very troubled by the impersonal machine which was the Arsenal, and the lack of care for the individual. All sorts of rumours went the rounds, of frequent suicides, of girls being blown to bits in the danger buildings, of men and girls being drowned in the canals on the marshes in the black-out, and even of girls being murdered. I knew that all these stories were just not true, but they formed the subject of much talk in the small hours, and were bad for morale. But it *was* true that at night girls who had had their meal in the canteen were turned out as soon as they had finished eating, and had nowhere except the factory to go to. Had they had rest rooms, the factory could have been cleared occasionally, and thoroughly ventilated. The air became so stagnant the girls would make their way to the lavatories, which were in a separate building, and sit there for long periods, until others at their table called them out to 'keep up the decimal'.

The girls in the tailor's shop were privileged because they were safe and well paid. If they complained, they knew they would probably be sent into the danger zone where, curiously, the money was less good than in our safe area. The reason for this was that for the work of the tailor's shop, girls' fingers were more nimble than men's, and the piece rates, which had been fixed for the men, were favourable for the girls. In the danger zone, where the work the girls did was often heavy, and where they were unable to work as fast as the men, their money was less each week. In the TNT factory, besides the danger of being blown to bits, the girls became yellow after a time, and were generally called 'canaries'.

Even in our test room conditions became worse and vermin multiplied. When a huge rat wriggled up the pipe under the washbasin, and flopped round our feet, I felt it was time to complain to the foreman. He only laughed, and said that girls need not worry as the rats could not climb up their legs, whereas they could climb up the trousers of the men and bite them in a vital place. He added that it was to prevent this happening that men in rat-infested areas wore string round each trouser leg; and he dismissed me with the remark: 'You know, you really aren't cut out for factory life.'

As I wrote in a letter, the chaos at the Arsenal gates, when coming on or going off duty, was appalling. As one left the Arsenal, one was likely to be 'tapped'; that is, an official put his hand on one's shoulder, and one had to follow him to a hut to be searched, to see that one was not carrying away any Arsenal property. This happened to me a few times, and was particularly irritating because it meant I missed my train, and consequently lost some precious hours of sleep. But one particular occasion about which I wrote made a great impression on me. It was pouring with rain and there was mud everywhere and puddles. By the side of the road up which we had to walk, and which of course was unlit, were deep trenches. It was pay night and, besides surging crowds of girls coming and going, a rowdy crowd of men were waiting for their pay. Suddenly four or five huge drays were driven right through this crowd, with the result that one girl was run over and badly injured, and one fell into the trench and broke her leg. My foreman was there at the time, and had picked the girls up, and later he showed me a letter he was writing to the 'Powers That Be', complaining of the conditions around the gates. If one mentioned lights, one was immediately believed to be a spy signalling zeppelins. In the period I was at the Arsenal nobody was hurt in a raid, but there were quite a few casualties in the dark. One girl coming from the canteen fell into a vat of boiling water and was killed. At the inquest, the Arsenal was censured for gross negligence; but it had no effect.

Working in the Arsenal had by now ceased to be an amusing adventure. I think the events I wrote about during the night of 15 October had changed it in my mind into a crusade. I felt I must do all I could to improve the conditions. I wrote a long letter to Miss Barker, and asked her if she would come and look at our factory, and see what could be done to improve it. She came, but it was no help, because the foreman and the forewoman went round with her, and had answers for everything, even as to why no-one was in authority on the night shift as I had told her in my letter. It seemed that welfare supervisors had no authority *inside* the factories; they were there for the girls to go to, but they never went to the girls.

I wrote everything out in a very long report, and decided to send it to Ramsay MacDonald, feeling that he would be sympathetic. For once my mother put her foot down, because there was such a prejudice against him on account of his peace activities. Mother was getting rather tired of me and my desire to reform the world, and used to say that things did go on quite happily before I appeared on the scene to put them right. So I kept my report, adding to it from time to time as I discovered what I considered new iniquities.

Esther was now working in the tailor's shop and in charge of a table glueing boxes for smoke charges. She told me a good deal about life in the shop and its difficulties. People talked a great deal about the money girls earned at munitions, but the real point is that they did *earn* it and no mistake. They worked at terrific pressure in the factory and for every minute's absence lost money.

In retrospect I suppose I had to dramatize my work somehow; and when I realized that I could no longer look on it as fun and excitement, I decided it was necessary to become a reformer. This led to my downfall, as will be seen later; but I continue with my letters to Norman.

London
17.11.16

Have you ever lived in a fool's paradise, and thought you were doing something well, and suddenly woken up with a shock to find you're a ghastly failure? I've just realized that all I have been writing to you about my success at the Arsenal was wrong. My boasted popularity is just because I'm easy and soft with the girls. The free atmosphere I was proud of is really lack of discipline. And other people are getting me out of difficulties because they think I'm incapable. I can't make up my mind whether to give it up, or stick it out until I get the sack. I have tried hard, but it's sheer ignorance and inexperience about organization which has got me down. The other PO told me this morning that each shift was getting a wigging for slackness, and mine was coming today. So every time the boss rings for me I expect it, and it gets on my nerves. I almost asked him for it last time I went up to his office.

The new food laws are good, though they ought to tackle the restaurants in the West End. If you walk down Regent Street or Oxford Street, and look in the shop windows, you would think all you read in the papers about the shortage of food was lies. But it isn't, for the poor people: they can't get all they want, and the rich get too much. I'd like to see food tickets for *everyone*. I feel blue today. As I was standing outside the gates, waiting for Hugh, last night, two women of about sixty, who have probably often seen me there, passed along. 'That thing always amuses me', said one. *I* was the thing, and somehow it made me want to cry. I don't like being a 'thing' that amuses people.

London
19.11.16

I've got my wigging, in the form of a letter. It said the room was in a disgusting state and never tidy, and too much time was wasted in argument, and we weren't to sleep on the braid. If things didn't improve, an example would have to be made. The boss is queer, he had it typed, then rang the bell, and gave it to me. Why couldn't he have said it? Of course, it's my fault. I get absorbed in the work, and forget the state of the room. I think the arguments apply to the other shift, but I've quarrelled with Reggie, because I had to tell him that he was lazy, and does only the minimum amount of work. He won't speak to me now, and does everything he can to annoy me.

Chartridge
25.12.16

I'm at Chartridge, because we have four days' holiday. I've decided to write a letter every Saturday to Miss Barker until something is done to improve our factory, and see if it has any effect. It was simply awful at the factory on our last night before the Xmas leave. They had a dance, which began decorously enough, with the boss leading off with the factory PO. But later it became a disgusting orgy, due to the men being so drunk. So I and most of the test room quitted, and went back to work. But it was worse in other factories, and as we went off in the morning, drunk girls—some quite young—were being carried away on stretchers. Hugh said that in one factory they had to disconnect the machines, as the men were so drunk they'd have done themselves harm had they tried to work them. Rather scandalous, isn't it? And they say it will be worse on New Year. I think Esther and I will ask for leave that night.

London
27.12.16

I'm writing this in the train; we've been in it for four hours. We took two hours to get down this morning; and at 4.30 they gave all of us who lived in Central London passes to go home because of the fog, as the railway couldn't guarantee any trains after that. We were twenty in our carriage, a rowdy crowd yelling at any train that overtakes us. I haven't written much about the journeys, but they are awful. We are always packed like this, and I keep writing and asking if we can't have some 'ladies only' carriages. The men use awful language (which doesn't matter really, of course) and talk the whole time of how much they are going to drink, or have drunk. One thing the Arsenal has done—it's made me anti-drink for ever.

London
29.12.16

We're so slack now, and it's difficult to keep discipline when there's so little to do. The trains are always late these days, and I can't get here on time, which is bad. The Soft Easy and Comfortable Railway—as it's called here—is supposed to run trains to get us here in time. The mice are worse than ever, and keep running over my feet as I work. If only their legs were longer and their tails shorter, I'd not mind them so much.

Yesterday, for the first time, they put on a 'Ladies Only' carriage. When we went to get in, it was full of men. So we called the guard, and he turned them out. One was especially offensive, and called me a 'bleeding sow'. One shouldn't mind being called names, but I was irritated. So, as he was getting out, I stuck my foot between his legs and he went flat on the platform. Today no men were in the carriage, but this man was waiting outside. As I put my hand on the side to get in, he slammed the door hard, and squashed my thumb. It didn't half hurt! Anyway, he won, because I did not really hurt him. It's difficult to write and I hope this is legible.

London
6.1.17

My birthday—and I'm twenty-five, which seems awfully old. And I've never done anything worthwhile—except get married. I saw an advertisement in the paper yesterday: 'Women over 25 wanted. No girls need apply.' That tells you! It's the sixth night of the week, and I'm tired. The lighting is so bad, that our eyes hurt when we do close work. They always say they'll improve it, but they never do. Counting the threads in fine material under a magnifying glass, which I help the girls do when we're slack, is very trying in this light. Sometimes it's chiffon, which is very fine. We only sample one tenth of the material which comes in. When I was running the machine which tests for tension, I had five miles of braid running through my hands. I think it's used on shells, to hold them by. I've had a letter from Miss Barker saying that something will be done to improve things, but I mustn't be so impatient. My thumb is better, but Esther had a bad time yesterday. A man barged between her and another man, and knocked her into the train, and hurt her so much that she cried all the way home. I was annoyed at this, and wrote to the Ministry of Munitions, warning them that, if something weren't done to stop this roughness at the station, they'd have a serious accident. I don't know if it was the right place to write to. I wear the Camel Transport Corps badge you sent me, and a woman in the factory asked what CTC stood for. When I told her, she said 'We thought it was the Church Temperance Club.'

It's absurd on day shift. The boss rings a bell when he wants any of us, and doesn't like to be kept waiting. One short ring is for me, two is for the boy, three for the clerk, four for the electrician, and one long one for Reggie. So as soon as it rings, we all jump up, and rush to the stairs leading to the office at once. It's queer being rung for like that.

London
25.1.17

It's terribly cold; but I'm one of the lucky ones. When I hear the girls talking in the train, and realize what they have to do before and after working here, many with children, and husbands away at the war, I feel I never ought to grumble again. They're wonderful! Hard work is good—I'll miss it when the war is over. And anyway, it absorbs my mind, and I can't think much about the terrible loss of life and destruction of the war, and my personal problem of being away from you, when life is all 'Plumstead and bedstead', as one of the Arsenal songs has it. But the memory of what the working women have to endure will, I hope, last with me for ever, and some day I'd like to help do something about it. I realize I'm really seeing the problems here, and not just talking about them and calling it 'socialism'. It's real—and terrible. I'm living with the problem, instead of just talking about it round the fire. What a contrast to my year in Cairo, and the effete, artificial life I lived there! It would be impossible to go back to that life again. There's a dignity about labour I never realized before, however much indignity there is about the way people have to live. The life here has saved me in time from the false values I was catching in Egypt, when I had to think of something to do to fill up the day, and make the hours pass. Anyway, I could never live a conventional life without a purpose again. Even if we have to live out east, there must be plenty of hard work, not just do-good meetings and committees, but achieving something, or I shall lose all my self-respect. What I'd like best would be to have something to do with schools, but I'm not trained enough to be a school-inspector—or even a teacher.

It was pay night last night, and I had the curious sum of £4 18s 0½d.

I'm afraid this will be in an OHMS envelope, as I've no others. When the boss gave them to me, he said: 'Don't use them for love-letters.' But a letter from a wife to a husband might be considered more as 'business correspondence' than 'love-letters'. —I'm sorry my writing is so indistinct. We used to get Hardmuth's Austrian pencils, and they were good; but now the supply of enemy pencils has run out, and we're using English ones, which are pretty poor. There's a PO in the factory whom I really hate. She's an ex-school teacher, and seems to hate me, too. We try not to see each other when we meet.

An ex-fire-engine horse here draws the van which brings up our stores. He always bolts when he hears a bell. One day another horse and cart got stuck, so they harnessed the ex-fire-engine horse to the other end of the cart, and rang a bell. He bolted at once, and pulled the other cart after him, and the horse as well.

2.2.17

I got so excited when I had your letter saying that, as you couldn't get leave to come home, I'd better come out on leave to you. And Mother went to the Foreign Office to ask if I could, with Uncle Herbert's help, and they said probably. But then she asked at Lloyd's about submarine danger, and they said, unless it were really necessary, they'd advise not, as the risks are very heavy. So I fear it's got to be no. What do you think?

One Arsenal song 'Slog on, slog on, and keep the decimal up', is sung to the tune of the Marseillaise. The decimal is all-important, more than the war. Workers in a factory are paid on a 'group Working', and each one in the groups has a certain number of shares, according to age, grade, etc. Each share in our factory and test room is worth 8d. If enough work is done, then it may be a 'two decimal'. Very occasionally it's a 2.5. Also, of course, they are paid a basic wage, and a fixed rate for overtime. No wonder Hugh has to have a hundred and fifty clerks to look after the wages of the women in the Royal Laboratory part of the factory (including our part) alone. There's a comb-out of men, and all those in the test room have been medically examined, and are very cross at all being A1. The girls keep congratulating them on being so healthy, but they hate being called up, not because they mind being in the forces, but because they'll get less. You can't think how much talk of money there is here! And they keep reckoning how much they should get each week, by this complicated system; and if they get a penny less than they expected, they are angry. Today the girls and men in my room have been having an edifying discourse on modern education in the elementary schools, and are unanimously of the opinion that it's all fad, and that the kids' heads are so stuffed up with rot that they won't be able to do a simple sum or write a decent letter when they leave. I just listen; but isn't our system of education 'for the poor' inadequate and undemocratic, compared to what those have who pay for it?

London
6.12.17

I'm worried about the men in my room. They now spend so much time talking to the girls, and stopping them from working. Sometimes they do nothing for twelve hours. They are supposed only to do the heavy work and not do anything the girls can do, and as there's practically no heavy work, they are idle. Whenever I complain to the boss, he says they'll be going into the army soon. And meanwhile they do nothing and are a nuisance.

I'm glad the Americans have come into the war. I'd hate to see them top-dogs after the war, just because they're rich and the rest of the world isn't. It seems wrong that they've been making profits out of the miseries of other nations. Now anyway we'll all suffer equally. Things are awfully bad. I wonder how long Germany can keep it up?

With the persistent cry for more men for the forces, it did seem curious that these men, all A1, should be kept in the Arsenal with literally nothing to do. But many curious things happened there. I could not understand why the boys in the test room, one of fourteen and one only thirteen, were allowed to work the same long hours, day and night, as the rest of us. The younger of the two, Alex, was an unusually intelligent child, who should certainly still have been at school. In the mornings, after the night shift, he would go to the swimming baths. In the factory, they had a number of boys from reformatories. Alex refused even to speak to them.

Despite some of the weaknesses of the welfare staff, I still wanted to join them, and was bitterly disappointed when I received no encouragement from Miss Barker. I should have realized that, as I was not being a success in the test room, I could not expect what amounted to promotion. Early in the New Year I decided to join a Trades Union, but I had no idea how to set about it. My sister-in-law, Cecil's wife, worked at Toynbee Hall, and knew Dr Mallon, who told her I should get in touch with Margaret Bondfield, which I did. She was most kind, and very helpful, and I immediately joined her Union, the National Federation of Women Workers, of which Mary McArthur was the Secretary, and Maggie Bondfield (as she was always called), the number two. I made the point, in talking to her, that as Socialists we should try and make the industries owned by the State, such as the Arsenal, better than the privately-owned industries. In talking to friends who were now working in munitions for firms not owned by the State, I found that with them conditions were far better than with us. I undertook to be branch secretary in the tailor's shop, and sign on as many girls as possible.

I'd written about the conditions to every Ministry in the least concerned, but nothing happened. And at the suggestion of my aunt, Mrs Ernest Franklin, I sent a paper on the conditions at the Arsenal to the National Council of Women, and they told me they were so impressed that they were really taking it up with the Government. But again nothing happened; 'there's a war on', was the invariable answer.

I became obsessed with writing letters. I wrote to Seebohm Rowntree, the head welfare officer at the Ministry of Munitions. He replied that, after the various accidents I had quoted, things had been put right. But I also warned him about likely further accidents on the trains, and when the shifts changed, and nothing was done about these dangers.

Curiously, at the Arsenal we did not then come under the Ministry of Munitions. I learnt this early on in my career as a Principal Overlooker. One day, a man came into the test room wearing a red band on his arm, with 'Ministry of Munitions' written on it. He asked me if he could see the specifications to which we worked in our testing, and I showed them to him, and explained how we worked them out from the tests. While I was doing this, the bell rang for me from the foreman's office. I raced up the stairs, to be met by a furious outburst. I was told that we, at the Arsenal, were directly under the War Office, and that our specifications must be kept a secret from the Ministry of Munitions, who were always snooping around, trying to discover them. And here was I, giving everything away. I had never seen the boss so angry. I insolently asked him if we weren't all fighting the same war, and whether it wasn't a good thing that we should all work to the same specifications. He just gave me a withering look, and rushed down the steps to turn the Ministry man out of the room. One good thing about this internecine warfare was that it helped one to forget the other war, which was seldom mentioned at the Arsenal. Mostly, the talk was of money. The workers were obsessed by it, I imagine because in their whole lives they had never had enough.

As time went on, I had another worry. Much of the stuff that came in was below standard, and I rejected it. Then I found the same material coming in again. I consulted the foreman, and he and the manager came and looked at the material which had reappeared after rejection, and told me that the manufacturers who made it had the monopoly, and that, if I kept on rejecting it, we should run short of material. So I had to agree to accept a lower standard. All this naturally reinforced my belief in Socialism, and my distrust of the Capitalist system.

One Sunday, when it had been freezing for a fortnight, I went skating on the Welsh Harp with my cousin Olive Franklin. She was working at the Fabian Society, doing research on Trades Unions, and I was naturally interested in talking it over with her. She told me of the latest ideas of Guild Socialism, evolved by G.D.H.Cole, and I was tremendously interested. And gradually I came to see that, if I became a welfare worker, I would be on the side of the bosses, and not on the side of the workers. So I decided to remain where I was for as long as they would have me. But I knew I was suspect, when two new 'girls' appeared in my room. One was the sister of the forewoman in the factory, and was there to report to her sister on my activities. The other was the sister-in-law of Miss Barker, who reported also what went on in my room. There was hardly enough work for the two of them.

Although I seemed to be so full of grievances, I was enjoying myself at the same time. The train journeys were amusing, with every woman or girl, whatever her age, being called 'dearie' or 'duck'. One of my girls (actually a married woman of over forty) asked me one day what sort of a husband I'd got. 'There's only two sorts', she said mournfully. 'Them as gets up and makes you an early morning cup of tea, and them as you get up and makes it for. I've got one of the wrong sort. I hope you have better luck, dearie.' It was as good a definition as ever I've heard.

When the thaw set in, the mud was indescribable, and got on everyone's nerves. The marsh-land on which the Arsenal was situated was below the level of the river, and at high tide the water ran back up the pipes and drains, and everything was swamped. And the constant firing of the big guns on the test range often broke our windows, and made our room cold and draughty. The man who came to mend the windows was coloured. One day he cut himself badly, and the girls all crowded round to see what colour the blood of a black man was. In some ways they were incredibly ignorant. They would often ask me about life in Egypt, and say how lovely it would be to marry a sheikh, and be the darling of the harem.

On the evening of 19 January, 1917, when Esther and I were crossing from Plumstead station to the Arsenal gates, and fighting our way through the crowds, a brilliant light appeared in the sky, followed by the noise of an explosion. 'Look out, it's in the danger zone', was the cry, taken up from mouth to mouth, and we all ducked our heads and waited. But nothing more happened, so we went on. A little later word went round that there had been a terrible explosion at Silvertown, the other side of the river, at the Brunner Mond explosive factory there. The boy Alex immediately asked permission to leave; and when I asked him what for, he said: 'To send a telegram to my mum to say I'm all right.' The rest of us found it difficult to settle, because rumours kept coming in of the tragic loss of life, and the chaos. Windows were broken as far west as Whitehall. My mother asked Hugh to telephone and find out if it was the Arsenal, as the explosion was heard at Porchester Terrace. As the night went on, messages came that any women whose homes were at or near Silvertown, who had left their children alone for the night, were to go to the office. Many of the married women would put their children to bed, and then come on night shift. And many of these children were found wandering dazed in the streets, and others were badly hurt. Those who were alive and unhurt were brought over to the garrison at Woolwich, and the mothers were taken there to identify them. Their friends became hysterical, and once again it was a nightmare in the factory. Nothing was said in the papers next day about the explosion. Great indignation was expressed in the Arsenal at such a dangerous factory being placed in an overcrowded working-class area, and wild rumours spread as to the number of killed and injured, until we believed that there were many hundreds, if not thousands.

Two months after the explosion, on 29 March, *The Times* gave an account of the findings of the Committee appointed by the Home Secretary to enquire into the causes of the explosion. Among other points, they stated that the fullest police investigation was unable to prove that it had been maliciously caused. Although this possibility could not entirely be ruled out, they were convinced no suspicion fell on any employee or other person concerned with the works. It was more probable that it was caused by a spark produced by friction or impact, or by spontaneous ignition due to decomposition.

In view of the exaggerated rumours which had been current as to the number of deaths caused by the explosion, they gave a correct account of all the casualties. Sixty-nine persons were killed on the spot, and ninety-eight were seriously wounded, of whom two died in hospital. Three hundred and twenty eight were slightly injured, and a further five or six hundred were treated on the spot for cuts and bruises. Of the ten men working on the shift at the time, only one remained alive. But of the ten women working on the shift, only one lost her life. The leading hand on the shift, and the police-constable on duty outside, were both posthumously decorated for outstanding courage.

Little is remembered of the explosion today, and as far as I can discover it is ignored in most accounts of the First War, although it probably caused the largest single list of civilian casualties in England of the whole of that war.

One Saturday, the weather changed, and spring seemed suddenly to be on us. In the dinner-hour I went out, and found a barrow-man at the gate selling daffodils. I bought some to put on my desk, and when I returned, and walked through the factory to my room, I found that the girls there had done the same; every table had a bunch of flowers, and even the machines had daffodils tied on at the side. It made the factory look happy and gay for once. We were all thankful that the long hard winter was over.

When the first Russian Revolution took place, we had less work to do, often not enough to last us for the shift. Munitions for Russia had been made in the Arsenal, and they were no longer needed. During the long idle hours, I would talk Trade Union propaganda to my girls, who had all joined, and even went so far as to recruit a large number of members in the factory itself. That was my undoing, as I tell in my letters.

London
4.4.17

I've got the sack. Sad, but true. I, who once gave select dinners for judges and titled ladies and paid gracious calls on the wives of advisers, and who is the wife of a brilliant lawyer, now a captain in the army, have been dismissed from the Arsenal for disobeying OF rule No.79, which states that a 'full day's work shall be done for a full day's pay'. Twice, for ten minutes each time, I have been discovered talking to the girls about Trade Unions, and collecting their dues, during work hours. Other POs may gossip, and read novels, and sign members for War Savings, during working hours, now that we've so little to do because of Russia. And nothing is said to them. They found they couldn't get me on the question of joining or encouraging others to join a Trade Union, because there's nothing in their blessed rule-book which allows them to do that. Of course, I've been a damned fool to lay myself open to this. When my boss found out, he wrote to the 'authorities', and they say I must be 'degraded'. The boss said I could work as a 'hand' in the factory, but I couldn't bring myself to do that while the present PO is there. Also, I told him, if I went into the factory, I could organize more girls in the Trades Unions, and then there'd inevitably be more trouble. So in the end it was decided that I should technically 'discharge myself', and leave at the Easter holiday, and no more would be said. What a ghastly failure I am! Seven months' hard work, and instead of promotion, as I had hoped, I get the sack. I felt pretty blue, and hadn't the courage to go straight home and confess. I wandered about the marshes in the dark for a long time, but eventually took a late train home. I found that Mother and Alice were very sympathetic, but I haven't yet dared to tell Father.

There's something queer about it all, as I know anonymous letters have been written about me. When I went in the next morning, two POs from the other shift met me, and said the boss had told them I was going for running a Trade Union. They were both furiously indignant, and on my side. Then an assistant foreman came up, and said he heard I was going because there was trouble in the Test Room—which is a lie. I then went to see Miss Barker. She really is a brick. She took me into her inner office, and gave me a cigarette—when I'd expected such a wigging. She said I didn't look like a criminal, and proceeded to make me an offer: to be a head-ganger in the shell factory, probably rising to be PO there in a month or so. But I knew I'd do the same thing again, if I found things bad in that factory, and I told her so. She said she hoped I'd not chuck the Arsenal altogether. I told her I was fed up about the anonymous letters, and she was very sympathetic. She then asked if I knew any chemistry, and when I said I did, she told me to discharge myself now, have a holiday, and she'd find me a job in the labs, where more women are wanted, to replace men. It will be more skilled and technical, no night work, and not such long hours. But I shall miss being with the 'girls'. Perhaps it's silly to take this easy way out, instead of going into the shell factory, but I felt I didn't want to get into any more trouble. She told me that the tailor's shop was one of the best factories and the others were far worse.

When I returned to the test room, I found that all the girls had gone in a body to the Manager, to complain about the way I'd been treated, and they threatened to strike. However, I talked them out of that. The men, too, were indignant, and all made pretty speeches, including Alex. At the end of the day, I said goodbye to the boss, who was most concerned for my future welfare, and when I told him what Miss Barker had suggested, assured me I was going to a very superior job, and one much better suited to my intellectual capacity!

Perhaps I should give up the Arsenal, and concentrate on Trade Union work instead but I don't feel quite keen enough, and still want to go on doing 'war work'. But I'm not really adjusted to factory work, because I find the pettiness and bullying unbearable. Frankly, I'm in a muddle, and I'll take a holiday and try to think things out. Uncle Herbert came in last night. He thinks I was right to want to improve conditions, but I'd blundered. Perhaps it was futile to try to get the girls to join the Union, when they know little or nothing of its purpose.

Ireland

19.4.17

Two letters have reached me here in Donegal—where I'm having a lovely time with Olive Franklin. One was from Miss Barker's sister-in-law. When the girls saw the boss, she wrote, he said I wasn't going for talking about Trade Unions (which is a lie!). They said how attached they were to me, and he said I was too easy-going with them; and the Manager had had a complaint from one of the girls about the unruliness in the test room. I've no doubt who that was—the sister of the PO from the factory, who worked in our room. I'd never heard anything about this, and it was mean to tell them one thing and me another.

The other letter was from the Trade Union organizer, saying how indignant they all were at the way I'd been treated at the Arsenal, and that they were going right into the matter of the procedure there, and would certainly not let it rest as it was. Perhaps I've not made quite such a fool of myself as I thought!

Two political points. Uncle Herbert, an ardent opponent of women's suffrage, has written a letter to his constituency saying that, although he is not a convert, yet he believes it is possible that the advantages of extending the franchise to women may in time outweigh the disadvantages, and that after due and lengthy consideration, he has decided to give his vote in favour of it! And there's talk of reforms in education, which seem good, if we can only get the money to carry them out. Education today in England is so inadequate, and is at the root of so many of our troubles.

London

29.4.17

I came back from Ireland yesterday, and went to the Arsenal in the afternoon to see Miss Barker. She gave me a letter to the head of the labs. He was out, but I saw the foreman, who was

103

nice, but surprised that I hadn't a degree or any experience in industrial or commercial chemistry. They have four girls there—two from Bedford College, who were distinguished students in my day. I went back to Miss Barker, to ask if, with my shady past, it would ever be possible to have a welfare job. She told me not to be stupid, and said I *had* no shady past, and had never done anything to be ashamed of. And she gave me letters to various welfare people, saying all sorts of nice things about my seven months' work. But she urged me to go and see the head of the chemical labs first. So this morning I went, determined to refuse the job even if it were offered me—but in the end I accepted, I think because he was such a charming person, with a nice twinkle. He began by saying he wanted me, but couldn't pay me the full amount yet, as I was inexperienced. But they've six men who have to be called up, and need girls to replace them at once, and that I'd be doing the patriotic thing by taking the job. *I* said I knew I wasn't good enough, and *he* said, if I'd ever worked in a lab at all, and knew the rudiments of chemistry, I was just the girl he wanted, as he could see I was quick and intelligent. I then said it was the human side of the work I liked best, working actually with the girls. He countered that by saying that, as the hours weren't so long, I could work in one of the many local clubs for women and girls in the evenings, and that his wife and daughters did that. He said I could do more good like that, than working alongside the girls in the factory, where I'd always be up against the authorities (I don't think he knew of my shady past).

I asked if he'd object to my doing Trade Union work, and he laughed, and said I couldn't convert *his* girls, as they were all that way inclined already, but that as he was a good old-fashioned Tory, I could start on him, and added: 'I expect you've an unsympathetic father at home. Girls like you always have.' Anyway, I couldn't hold out any longer, and now it's only got to be approved by the 'military authorities', and I'm to start right away. I only get £2 a week to start with, and more for overtime. No 'time' tickets to pick up, and a holiday with pay after six months. I'll be a metallurgist in the Gun & Carriage Factory Chemical Laboratory, and I think test iron ores used in the various guns. Later, I went to see the Trade

Union people who are quite agitated about what was done to me, and are taking it up with the head of the Arsenal. They offered me a job as a Trade Union Organizer, to go and speak all over the country. But I'm now pledged to the Arsenal!

Next day I behaved stupidly, and went with the local Trade Union Organizer distributing pamphlets at the Arsenal gates. But I wasn't caught, and it has nothing to do with what followed. The following day I started working in the labs, and enjoyed it very much. But that evening, Hugh rang up and said the Superintendent of the Arsenal had said I wasn't to go back again because of my 'Bolshevik tendencies'. I'd had the chance of staying on in the test room in a lower job (which they hadn't really offered me!), so I couldn't come back to work in a better job. Then Hugh proceeded, over the 'phone, to give me a real dressing-down, all about how rottenly I'd behaved, and how it wasn't *my* business to try and reform the Arsenal, and how seriously I'd compromised him, as he'd recommended me, and how all the staff were talking about me and him, and how he was having trouble with his men that week, and a threatened strike on his hands, and if I didn't clear out of the Arsenal for good and all, and stop my Trade Union work there too, *he'd* have to leave. It was a regular slating. So I thought it best to cut everything; I didn't want to complicate things for him, as he's so happy and settled in his work, after all the complications of his suffrage days. The Trade Union people were going to have questions asked in the House about tyranny in the Arsenal, but I've told them to drop the whole thing.

And this morning I went off to Alice's office, to sign on for the Land Army. I hope I shan't compromise *her,* as she has a high-up post at the Board of Agriculture. But I'll try and join the Agricultural Workers Trade Union.

As a footnote to this, I will add my contact, some seventeen years later, with the head of the laboratories. I was then a member of the LCC Education Committee, and chairman of the governing body of the King's Warren School, a secondary girls' school at Plumstead. And Mr Mundy, the man who had been so charming to me at the laboratories, was my vice-chairman. He recognised me at once, but I never realized who he was until one day, when I disagreed with him over something, he said: 'You know, one day I'll really have to tell the girls of the school about your past at the Arsenal.' So I told them myself, and I think they were impressed.

———

1917—1918

The Land Army (1)

I never carried out my intention of being active in the Trade Union whilst I was in the Land Army. I wrote to the National Union of Agricultural Workers, and from their reply I gathered they were not very interested in having women as members, and were doing little to recruit the Land Girls. I wrote back that as this was the case I saw no point in becoming a member. I then received a postcard saying: 'Don't stand outside and throw stones. You can join us if you want to.' Probably I was wrong, but I did no more about it. I had a lurking suspicion that, if I became involved, I might cause as much embarrassment to my sister Alice as I had to my brother Hugh. She was very happy in her work, at the Ministry of Agriculture, and very popular.

When I went to be interviewed, I was asked if I would be willing to be a peripatetic Group Leader, to be paid 25s a week. I agreed. I was to be attached to one county. First I would have to see the local farmers, and persuade them to employ a gang of women for field-work, to replace their men. Then I had to canvass the district, find the women willing to be employed, start them off on the job, find someone to lead the gang, and then go on elsewhere and collect a new gang. That was the theory, but generally I could find no one willing or capable of being a gang leader, so I often had to stay with the gang the whole time they were on this particular piece of work; while I was doing this, the farmer had to pay me my 25s. Some of the farmers were very difficult to persuade, and some refused outright. I found the best propaganda came from the farmer who was pleased with his gang

107

telling others about us on market days. When I had no gang, or when it was too wet for field-work, I had to visit all the local farmers, persuading them to employ Land Girls, at the princely sum of 18s a week, for work in the dairy, the stables, or in the fields. These girls were trained at specially selected training farms. I was used as a kind of guinea-pig, because, if the farmer was courteous and polite to me, I could recommend him as a good employer of girls. But if he were too familiar, and made unpleasant suggestions—as some of them did—he was black-listed. Later on I became a Welfare Worker, whose job it was to visit the girls in their billets, organize their spare time, and deal with any complaints.

In every village there was a voluntary registrar, whose duty it was to help look after the Land Girls, and to whom I reported as soon as I arrived anywhere, to find out all about the local farmers. These registrars were almost always kind, human people. Some were the wives of the squires or big land-owners. Some the wives of the clergymen. Some were retired school-teachers, and at least one I met was the delightful wife of a publican. I stayed, in my wanderings, with many of these registrars, and met many extremely interesting people in this way. A District Organizer, a paid post, was in charge in the County town, with various paid and unpaid helpers.

The farm I was sent to for training was at Buckland, in Berkshire. It was run by a voluntary organization for placing volunteers on the land, who in the early days were less tied to working for the duration of the war than the National Service Land Girls. I already knew a good deal about the less skilled side of farm work, as we had always been encouraged to help at busy times on my father's farm at Chartridge. But it was thought wise that I should have a very brief professional training. Whilst I was at Buckland, I heard that Norman had been wounded in action, in his head. I was naturally very anxious about this, as I tell in my letters, and felt guilty at having left Cairo, and not being there to look after him in his convalescence. But he soon recovered, and had plenty of kind friends to take my place.

I tell the tale of my training and my early work in the letters to Norman that follow.

Buckland
5.5.17

I'm very happy here, though after my last job, this is a very cushy one. I'm living at the school-house with a garrulous school-mistress and a deaf school-master. They object to smoking in the rooms, but otherwise it's all right. We have all our meals with other trainees at the Lodge, and sit there in our spare time, only sleeping in our billets. There are 12 trainees, the older ones rather boring, and the younger ones school-girlish. One other girl is in my billet, fairly nice, but wears ear-rings on the farm, and is a bit common. We wear mufti when not on the job. Today—Saturday—is only a half-day's work. I had to be at the farm to groom the horses by 6, breakfast at 8, and from 9.15—12.30 hoeing beans. I think the advantage of this training, which won't teach me any new skills I hadn't learnt at Chartridge, is that it teaches me to stick steadily at a job without leaving off. In the afternoon I walked four miles into Farringdon with some of the other girls, to have tea at a shop. But, because of the Devonport rationing, we were only allowed two ounces of flour food each to eat. I, being a lawyer's wife, found a way round the Law, because Lord Devonport had nothing to say against our buying as many buns as we liked, and we ate them under a hedge on the way back. This was necessary, as we'd missed the 5.30 tea at the Lodge, and would have had nothing more all the evening except cocoa at 8—and we get very hungry. We have much more than our ration of flour for our meals, because I suppose they have to do it as cheaply as possible, and they fill us up with bread.

Buckland
8.5.17

I've been spreading muck all day, and it's a messy job. The farmer told me to ride back on the cart-horse, but it was so big and wobbly, I ignominiously fell off. I find I only have to get up to groom the horses at 6 every other day; alternate days I don't start till 9, and we knock off at 4. We have a week in the dairy, a week with the poultry, a little ploughing and harrowing, and the rest of the time is spent hoeing or carting muck, for which we are paid 3d an hour—1d less than the villagers. It's said in the village that the owner of the estate has

109

a good business head, to get as much work as possible done cheaply in the name of patriotism.

Buckland
13.5.17

I was very upset when I got the telegram saying you were wounded. I went up to the big house to telephone to Mother, otherwise I'd have had to bicycle four miles into Farringdon. The lady of the house had given orders that the Land Girls weren't to use the 'phone, and although I sent in the telegram, she wouldn't let me. But the parlourmaid took pity on me, and let me use the one in the pantry, standing by to see I didn't run off with anything—Mother is finding out what she can from the War Office.

I've been ploughing the last few days, and am now doing it quite well. It's not hard work, just knack, and knowing how to manage the horses. The bailiff rode up on his horse to watch me the first day, and said I was pushing the plough so hard, I could do without the horses. Now I don't push, only guide. A lot of girls take ploughmen's jobs, and I should actually like that. But if I'm to be a group leader, as I've undertaken to be, I won't plough, or milk, or do anything skilled—just collect groups for the unskilled work. But I'm glad I came here; I'm enjoying it all very much. The instructress here says I'm very good at ploughing and harrowing, and even the men I work with say so too. And I can ride the farm horses now without falling off. Even in the rain and thunderstorms we've been having I'm loving it all. I'm also working in the dairy. I don't much like milking—it's so stuffy and smelly having to keep one's head under the cow for so long at a time, and they're unattractive beasts compared to horses. I hear I'm to be a group leader in Herts, though I'd prefer to be a carter.

Hatfield
31.5.17

It's simply killing here. I'm the only inmate in a newly-opened hostel, with an elderly matron in charge, a very prim old maid. As soon as I arrived, she asked me if I wouldn't like to change out of my breeches! But as I'm alone, she gives me just what I like to eat; and I have a large room to myself, and a bath

110

whenever I want one. It's a bit dull in the evenings, but it's only for a week. I'm working in a gang for the time being, eight hours, but I hope to get my group-leader's job soon.

Barkway
3.6.17

I'm in digs here, and I think I've struck gold again. I'm billeted on an oldish widow in a rambling gabled house, and have a very large sitting-room all to myself, and an equally large bedroom. There's a local registrar—a voluntary job—in the village, and a district supervisor three miles away at Barley, who is Redcliffe Salaman's secretary. [Dr Redcliffe Salaman, FRS, a research chemist as well as a country squire, was a friend of my parents, and also of Norman.] And when she came to see me, she brought me messages to go over to the Salamans whenever I'm free. Now I must make a confession: I bought a motor-bike my last day at Hatfield, quite a small one. I wasn't allowed to get on it until I had bought it. Then the man showed me how to start it, and I rode gaily up the Great North Road, until I realized he hadn't shown me how to stop it, and I didn't know which was the brake. So I had to stop it by dragging my feet on the ground—fortunately my land-army boots are very thick. I came up here on it quite happily. It's a bit lazy at times, and sits down and sulks on the hills; so I have sometimes to get off and push it. But that's because I don't yet quite understand the throttle. On one hill I found two Land Girls who helped me push; they were the first National Service Land Girls I've seen. I'm proud at doing this run so soon after buying the bike, even though I did have to do some pushing, and am a bit bruised from falling off. It's a Levis. Mother seems reconciled to it, though, when I 'phoned to say I'd bought it, she seemed a bit upset. I've sent her a telegram to say I've arrived safely. I got so sick of the push-bike.

Barkway
5.6.17

This *is* some job. I've got to collect a gang to work for a farmer who is boycotted—but nobody tells me why this is. As soon as I collect women for the gang, someone goes along and tells them not to work for him. We are supposed to start tomorrow, and all I've got for the gang at present is one old man, who is a retired butler, and two idiot girls! I've been visiting lots of women with the local registrar, with no luck. It's a queer village: the people are very modern, and have a wholesome dislike of the marriage tie. Few of those I've visited are 'Mrs', but nearly all have lots of children. The farmer we're to work for is an educated man. His fields are in an awful state. If we can't get the women, I'll try for a gang of school-children on Saturday. Besides the immorality, there are an unusual number of village idiots. And living conditions seem worse than in Whitechapel. It's because the educated farmer is contemptuous of the uneducated women that they boycott him—I believe. So I'll start visiting them all over again, to say they'll never deal with him, only with me. And that's the condition I'll make for working for him. It's a year today since I last saw you.

Barkway
9.6.17

Although the farmer is very difficult with the women, I get on well with him—very well. He doesn't want me ever to be lonely in the evenings, so he comes along to see what I'm doing. Today I've been having tea with him and tomorrow lunch. He says I'm to ask him for anything I want, and not to be shy about it. I really want to ask for a bath—the one in my billet is only a stand-up thing in the sitting room. But I haven't dared yet. He's very old-fashioned, and might be shocked. He goes everywhere on a beautiful horse. If I could ride well enough, he'd lend it to me. But I can't—so he gave me a whole can of petrol for the motor-bike instead. Just how he has it to spare, I wouldn't know, and with the present stringent rationing, I'd better not ask. His wife is a very reserved person, who hardly talks. She's terribly distressed because her 19-year-old son is missing, probably killed.

The gang isn't so bad after all. We were eleven today, excluding the two idiot girls, who got on my nerves, so I've dispensed with them. It was pay-day today, and it seemed so funny to take money from him when I went to tea, that I told him he'd better pay me for the whole time when I leave. He was afraid I'd be hard up, and was quite relieved when I said I wasn't. I was sent on my bike to another village last night, to

112

see if the farmers would employ a gang of women. But the
local Land Army registrar says they all refuse; so many men in
the district are exempted, that they have all the male labour
they want. The registrar is the wife of the local parson, and he
thanked me for going there, as he said it was a joy to see such a
healthy specimen of humanity these days!

Barkway

10.6.17

I hear the mail home went down last week, so I've no letters
from you. I've found out about the petrol. The farmer was
given it by the Government to work a machine for grinding
corn for the pigs; but at the same time it brought out an order to
say that no corn may be ground for the pigs! *So* he passes the
petrol to me. I like people who aren't above mild lawbreaking!

Barkway

12.6.17

Standing for seven hours a day in a field without shade,
chopping thistles, is pretty strenuous in the heat we are having
at present. I look very odd, because I wear a blue sunbonnet!
The farmer is turning very human, and lets us work as a gang
any seven hours we like. So we've chosen from 9.30 to 12.30
and 4.30-8.30 pm. I can't think why he was boycotted; but of
course he's a snob, and I suppose I oughtn't to like him. He
said once that his horse was more refined and better bred than
any of the village-women, and much more worthwhile spending money on! It's amusing to like people and disapprove of
them at the same time.

When the farmer heard that a friend of yours from your
division was in London, and coming to tea with Mother, he
told me to go to London and stay the night. I motor-biked to
Cambridge, and took the train from there. I'd forgotten my
wedding-ring, which I never wear on the farm, and got 'off' on
the train with a Trinity House pilot who takes boats through the
mine-fields in the North Sea. He asked me to go along and
have tea with him, but I was in a hurry to get home. I enjoyed
meeting your friend, and hearing all about the battle of
Gaza—what a muck-up it was for us—and his adventures
being shipwrecked on the way home. Incidentally, it was the

first time I'd worn my Land Army breeches in London, and I felt quite self-conscious walking through the streets. There was a bad Zeppelin raid that night, so I stayed at home, and caught the 5.55 back in the morning.

They had a terribly bad raid recently, in the day-time. A bomb was dropped in the classroom of a school in Poplar, and another fell among a crowd waiting for a bus at the Minories. These horrors make everyone feel sick. I do wish they wouldn't talk about reprisals. It's just as cruel to kill German babies as English ones. What will it benefit us to win the war if, in doing so, we lose our sense of humanity? And I wish we weren't always talking about what we'll 'take' when the war's over. We're as bad as the Germans and the Russians and all the rest of them. Last night I went over to the Redcliffe Salamans; the Zangwills were there. And all this talk about 'when England has taken Palestine' seemed wrong. Anyway, this talk of all that the British will do for the Jews when they *do* have Palestine may make the Turks and Germans harder on the Jews there than they would be otherwise.

Barkway
16.6.17

I'm in a fix. The farmer now says he doesn't want a permanent gangleader, because he hasn't enough work for a gang, but I can't get anything very definite out of him. I've a notion he's not as pleased with us as he was. The thistles, which grow in between the rows of the corn, are so thick in the last field we did, that I think we left a lot behind. So yesterday, being Sunday, I motor-biked to Ware, to see Miss Pullar, who is the District Organizer of the Land Army in Herts. She lives in a very 'County' house, in a park. She says I'm to stay here a week longer and then go to the other side of Herts, the more suburban side with less nice country, but with the advantage of being fairly near Chartridge.

Barkway
20.6.17

It's a year today since I left Cairo, and I've achieved very little in that year, except gain experience—always useful. I talk to my farmer a lot about Socialism and Trade Unions. He just

114

smiles, and says the perfect Englishman is the product of the hunting field, and if it weren't for all that the Englishmen of the upper classes have learnt through hunting, where would we be today, by Gad, and all *that*. And yet we're very good friends, which is odd. He has just given me another can of petrol, so I'm motor-biking home for the weekend.

Stocks Aldbury
29.6.17

I left Barkway this morning. I was really sorry to leave. I took a tender farewell of the gang; the corn's grown too high for any more hoeing. And I feel quite a success, as I've made them all keen to work again for this particular farmer in the future. Also, he's very well-known among the farmers in this part of the country, at the markets and sales, and he keeps telling the others how well the gang has worked, and it will probably make some more of them ask for the same thing, and this is what I exist for. I motor-biked here, nearly fifty miles, and only had to push the thing twice. I find this place very frightening, as there's a butler, who looked on me with terrible contempt, and said 'Is this all, Madam?' when he carried in, at arm's length, my rucksack, and a cardboard box fastened to the back of the bike, with a dress for evenings. It's the home—a large one—of Mrs Humphrey Ward, and her daughter is the registrar here. She seems very nice and kind, though I'm rather scared of her, too. But it's very kind of them to ask me to stay. Apparently, I'm to go round calling on farmers who don't want to employ women, asking them to take on gangs of women who don't want to work, supervised by gang-leaders sent by the Board of Agriculture whom they've not been able to recruit. Some job! I wish I'd read some of Mrs Ward's books!

Tring
2.7.17

I left Mrs Ward's this morning. They were all terribly kind to me, and I've instructions to go there whenever I want a bath or a bed or company. I felt embarrassed at not having read any of Mrs Ward's books. Mr Ward kept filling my pockets with cigarettes. Miss Dorothea Ward is a dear; she found me this billet where I'm staying now. I'll not be as spoilt as I was at Barkway, or as luxuriously pampered as I was at Stocks. It's a little villa, on the outskirts of Tring, owned by a young couple. Although the woman thought I could live with them, and despite my theoretical Socialism! I've persuaded her to give me the 'best' parlour as my sitting-room. I just can't bear having meals with people with whom I must keep up a polite conversation all the time, and with whom I've nothing in common. Of course I'm a snob; I loved having meals with the family, and good talk, at Stocks. The man here works in a mill, and I haven't anything to say to him. I'm ashamed of myself—but it's nice to be by myself in the evenings.

At the moment I've a gang of five, and say that's enough, for they work harder while they're at it than the last gang. And it's a harder job, pulling out docks with our hands. It makes my back ache, and my hands torn and sore. But I expect I'll soon get used to it. I wish you could see my gang. Two very respectable young married women and one respectable older one, who used to be a servant in London. She's very tall and lean. A slovenly, dirty low-caste girl of seventeen and —the prize of the lot—a hugely fat swarthy old woman, Mrs Smith, who wears a hat all the time with an ostrich feather, and ear-rings, and is a regular gypsy. She told me that when she was young she lived in Aylesbury, but from April to November wandered round the country with her mother and brothers, mainly in Middlesex and Kent, potato-setting, harvesting, fruit picking, hopping, and coming home for the winter. She talks to the docks as she picks them, saying: 'Come on, dearie, it's no good your hiding behind that thistle, Smithie sees you', and keeps me in fits of laughter. I have never seen such neglected fields as those we are now working in, and what makes the work more difficult is that it should have been done two months ago. Now the ground is so hard, the dock-roots have grown down so deep, and the corn is so high, it makes us ache all over. As one woman said today: 'It's farmers like that, with these neglected fields, that help make the bread so dear.' For the fields only grow about a third of the wheat which they should do. I think the Board of Agriculture should inspect these fields thoroughly. After work yesterday, I called on the farmer where we're to move to next. The farmer, his wife, two

116

children, a servant girl and two friends were all having tea in the kitchen, and asked me to join them. They weren't able to place me at all. Everyone here takes me for a North-country girl, because I haven't a Herts accent. I tell them my father has a small farm the other side of the hills and they take me as being like themselves, which they wouldn't do if I said I came from London, and was the wife of a lawyer!

Tring
10.7.17

It rained so hard yesterday that we couldn't work in the fields, so I thought I'd go up to London to see my bosses—the Board of Agriculture and Fisheries Food Production Dept, Women's Branch, where Alice works. I bravely went in my farm-kit breeches, thick boots, leggings and waterproof tunic to my knees. I was interviewed by Miss Meriel Talbot, the head of the whole department, who is very practical and business-like, and Mrs Alfred Lyttleton, a charming person, kind and sympathetic, lovely to look at, but with not the vaguest or remotest idea of land-work, probably thinking it just consisted of ploughing and reaping and milking and collecting eggs. But she wanted to know everything I'd been doing, asked searchingly about the billets I'd had, and whether there were bathrooms. When I said no, she wanted to know how I managed! I didn't tell her I could wash just as clean in a pint of hot water as in a luxury bath, once I knew how, and just as all-over too, because I didn't think information like that would be useful to someone as elegant. She was concerned that my fingers were bound up in plaster, because of the sores from docking, and told me to be careful not to get blood-poisoning. The third person I saw was Miss Kindersley, very nice, also, and to her I poured out my problems of the farmers who refused to employ the gangs, and how they had too many soldiers doing work which women could quite well do, and how others just left their land dirty. She asked if I thought I might be more useful elsewhere, but I'm determined to get more farmers to take us on here.—I like it here, it's so near home!—I gave her a few ideas, and said the B of A inspectors ought to be able to *make* farmers clear their land properly, and tell us where the dirty farms were and insist on the farmers

117

employing us. She kept saying it was no good being so critical, but five minutes later repeated all I'd said as her own idea, and gave me no credit for it!

It was a privilege to meet three such outstanding women as Mrs Humphrey Ward, Mrs Alfred Lyttleton and Miss Meriel Talbot. Mrs Ward was a most generous hostess, and I took advantage of her invitation to turn up any time I was in the district and wanted a bed or a meal. She was the niece of Matthew Arnold, and her novels were serious. Many of them carried a religious message, notably *Robert Elsmere*. I wonder if anyone reads her books today? I must confess I never found them easy reading when I read them later. But in the days when I knew her she was writing novels of a more popular kind. During dinner in the evening she would question me closely about all I had done during the day, about my curious gang, and their lives. She must have written down at once all that I told her, because soon after two of her books appeared with a Land Girl as heroine, and one was partly made up of letters which the girl wrote to her husband at the front.

I was amazed to find that two such intelligent women as Mrs Ward and her daughter Dorothea were quite violently opposed to women's suffrage. They felt so keenly about it, that it was difficult for someone as raw as myself to argue with them. Later on, I was staying with them when the Bill giving the vote to women over the age of eighteen was passed by the House of Lords. They had been to London that afternoon to listen to the debate, and came home, both of them actually in tears, because they felt their cause had been betrayed by Lord Curzon. Mrs Ward said to me at dinner: 'I suppose you and your generation are now happy', and I felt quite guilty at rejoicing when she genuinely minded it so much. I met many interesting people at her house, including her daughter Janet, and her son-in-law, George Trevelyan; and the Bishop of London and Mrs Creighton. But although I found it easy to talk to Mrs Ward and Dorothea, I was usually tongue-tied before their visitors. Many years later I worked with Dorothea in the work she did for disabled children, and with her and Mrs Trevelyan at Coram's Fields, which Mrs Trevelyan had been successful in saving from the builders for the children of London.

It was Mrs Ward who first started play-centres for the children of London, to give them places to play, under skilled leadership, in the evenings and the holidays. I was glad when the LCC took them over, and that I then had much to do with their organization and development. She also started the settlement which bears her name in Bloomsbury, where also in later days I had many contacts. She was a great woman, and will probably be remembered more for her pioneering social work than for her novels. Mr Ward was always kind to me, and would come and see me off in the mornings on my motor-bike. He had the endearing habit, when anything particularly agitated him, of saying: 'I must write to *The Times* about it', and would send off his letter post-haste.

Mrs Alfred Lyttleton was lovely to look at, and invariably kind and considerate. She wanted to know all about Norman, and would listen with an appearance of real interest, and in return tell me about her son Oliver. She was a great humanizing influence in the Land Army, and any girl privileged to come in contact with her was immediately enthralled. Miss Talbot had a quick and ready mind, as well as a ready wit. I think she was the brains of the organization. I envied my sister working in close contact with two outstanding women. As I was working within easy distance of London, and as Alice was one of the staff, I was often sent for to give my views, and enjoyed my excursions there. Miss Talbot would at times wear Land Army uniform, and as she was tall and slim, looked very charming in it. Sometimes, with older members of the Land Army, it was difficult to persuade them to wear the uniform. Later at a gathering of Welfare Officers, when Miss Talbot was impressing on them the necessity of wearing the uniform, as an example to the girls, she said: 'Of course, if anyone has bandy legs, we would understand that they would not want to wear it.' After that, there was no difficulty.

To return to my letters from Tring:

Tring
12.7.17

It's terribly hot. Because some fools in Parliament suggested putting the clock on an hour, we lose an hour's work a day, and an hour's pay. They can organize offices and schools and railways, etc, but they can't organize the sun. The dew makes it impossible to work in the fields till 9.30 am—new

119

time—when we used to start at 8.30 am—old time. And we have to leave off at 4.30—new time—because the mothers want to be home when the children come back from school. Else they're afraid they'll fall in the canal, or the reservoirs. My friend Mrs Smith didn't turn up to work today till after dinner. She said she'd got drunk last night, because it's such thirsty weather, and anything less than three pints is no good at all, and so she didn't 'feel for' work this morning.

Yesterday there was great commotion in the gang. One of the very respectable young married women made rude remarks about Mrs Smith, calling her a dirty old woman. Mrs Smith was naturally annoyed, and said in an impressive voice: 'You're not to say things like that about me. May you have triplets when your husband comes home'. The other woman was rather shocked and said: 'Not me. It would kill me.' 'Then I'll come and lay you out', replied Mrs Smith. At this the other woman shouted: 'I wouldn't want your dirty hands on me when I was dead. You'll do no such thing', and went off and lay under a hedge and cried. Mrs Smith was equally upset. 'What's wrong with me laying her out', she cried. 'I lay out everybody around here, and it's the first time anyone said a thing like that', and went off and cried under another hedge. I was in fits of laughter, but thought I must get them at work again. So I went to the young woman, and told her not to be silly. She said: 'They do say she has the power of wishing things on you, and I don't want to have triplets. I know it would kill me.' I assured here that Mrs Smith really wasn't a witch, but just an ordinary gypsy, and in the end made her see sense. Then I went to Mrs Smith, and told her not to worry, as I was sure she was a most competent layer-out. In the end they made it up, and we went on with the work.

Mrs Smith told me one day that her first husband was a chimney sweep, and when he fell down a chimney and hurt his back, he'd been ill till he died, and for 'the best years of my life I had to stick with him, as we were married. But the next time I knew better, and I've never married the man I live with now.' She certainly adds to the amusement of gang work.

Another of the gang, who's looked on as a bad young woman, quarrelled with some of the others, and has left to be a barmaid.

120

I've now found a farmer at Aldbury to take us on. I visit farmers on the bike after the day's work. Some farmers ask for regular Land Girls, and when I ring up headquarters and ask for them, they say they haven't any. What's the use of this propaganda to persuade people to use Land Girls if there aren't any?

I'm quite falling in love even with this part of Herts—the narrow leafy lanes, the odd little streams, the peaceful, prosperous-looking farms, and the villages with the cottages clustered round the village greens. And the market-towns with their old-fashioned high-streets, and the bye-ways and court-yards which are quite unchanged since Queen Elizabeth's day. It's all so homely and simple. But I can't help getting pretty depressed sometimes. The war just goes on and on, and there's no chance, you say, of your coming home even for a short leave. I've just got to go on pulling up docks! But the farmer was quite pleased when he paid us, because we'd pulled up thistles as well as docks and he'd only engaged us to pull up docks! I'm leaving this gang next week, to start another one for a farmer further off, this time hoeing out the weeds between rows of young roots.

In the evening I called on the registrar of the Land Army in Hemel Hempstead, and she gave me supper, and then sent me on to see a gentleman farmer who wanted a gang, and I got home very late—and haven't yet got lights on the motor-bike. But I got home all right. I'll confess I get scared in lonely country lanes after dark, and that's why I've not yet got any lights. But I'll have to get used to them in the winter. I'm also scared in London traffic. I'm not at all courageous! On Saturday I went to see fourteen farmers and three lady registrars about gangs. The farmers all had village women working for them already, so they didn't need me to start a gang. But I've now visited all the farmers in the district—'Hemel Hempstead rural'—and am glad to have cleared them all. I'll write a report about it to my Hertford office. Then I biked over here to Chartridge for the night—and a real bath.

Tring
17.7.17

Tonight I'm tired—something has gone wrong with the

motor-bike, so I've had to hire a push-bike, and go over to Berkhamstead and other places seeing farmers. I had to try and persuade them to employ Land Girls—some say they'll take me, but not anybody else they haven't seen. I'm not in the market. One dear old farmer of eighty was most interesting, and reminisced for ages about the 'good old days', and finally said he'd take a girl in three weeks for the harvest. Like many other farmers round here, he refused to change the time, and talked of that 'damned maggotty government in London'. Another place, in a large park, was run by a rich widow, very pleasant, who gave me lots of strawberries and cream. I got home quite late again.

There's been a real tragedy in Long Marston. The far-mer—who had asked to see me today—went up to London to sell his eggs, and in the evening his barn and farmsheds and some cottages next door were all burned down. Everyone in the district rushed to help, and then it was discovered the farmer's only child, a boy of seven, was nowhere to be found. Early next morning they found the body in the stable, underneath his dead pony. He still sent word for me to go and see him, and he looked ghastly. It's rather like a Hardy story, this miserable tragedy in a lovely, peaceful village.

Chartridge
14.8.17

I wonder what you think of the idea of a Jewish Battalion. Father went to the meeting yesterday to oppose it, but they seem to be fairly far on with it. Personally, I think it a mistake, because I think Jews ought to fight for the country of which they are nationals. Supposing the Germans also had a Jewish Battalion? And it may make the Turks behave worse to the Jews in Palestine. I do hope you won't join it!

I've just finished my holiday, which I spent with the Girl Guides here in camp.—You write about my being scared of the butler at Mrs Ward's; he and I got quite friendly later. In his off-moments he was a 'National Guard'. Their lady's maid was a dear old thing, who used to doctor the blisters on my hands and heels, which I get from my hard labours. When I called on the Mayor and Mayoress of Hemel Hempstead, they tried to show me out by the back-door, but I wouldn't go that

122

way, and told them I always used the front-door! They're the only people I've met so far who've been really snobbish and stuck-up.

Chartridge
16.8.17

I'm staying at Chartridge, and going over to the farm near Tring every day. Yesterday it was too wet to work, so after two hours' flirtation with the charming bachelor farmer of forty-five, for whom I'm now working, I went to the Labour Exchange at Watford, to see if I could pick up any 'gang' workers. My bike's going well now; I did forty miles on half a gallon of petrol. In the evening, I was walking along the canal at Tring, when a barge came along, and the bargee asked if I'd like a lift. I jumped at it, and had fun steering the barge. Mother was shocked when I told her! When I was at the B of A in London, I asked them what I should do when it was too wet even for going round on the bike, and they suggested I should write amusing accounts of my gangs for the B of A leaflets. I'm afraid it shows they don't take me or my work very seriously. I've now invested in real waterproof overalls for riding the bike, just like a man's.

Today I've been pulling weeds in the wurzels for six and a half hours, and my back and legs are one big ache. I'm sorry you've been found fault with for being untidy. Actually, I'd bought you a very special shaving outfit, and brushes and a looking-glass, for a wedding-day present, before I'd had your letter about the telling-off.

Chartridge
19.8.17

I've been having a strenuous time. On Friday, I went off on the motor-bike to my wurzels at Tring, and about two miles from the farm the belt of the bike came off, and I had to push the wretched thing to the garage and get it mended. Fortunately, it was mostly down-hill, and in the steepest parts I sat on it and coasted. But I arrived at work at 10.30 instead of 9. When I got home, there was a telegram telling me to go to Welwyn, right the other side of the county. It was pouring with rain, but I started off at 8.30 next morning with my night-things and my dinner on the carrier, ready for all emergencies. I'd first to call on the Countess of Cavan, at Ayot St Lawrence, near Wheathampstead. It's lovely country round there, completely rural, although so near London. It's quite near Lamb's Mackery End. The Countess was very unconventional. She lives in a small house, and apparently without servants. Her nephew of fourteen opened the door, and I went into a pretty drawing-room, where there was another boy and an old lady. Then the Countess and another woman came in, and everyone was very friendly. I was in my waterproof outfit, with a sou'wester, caked from head to foot in mud, and sat in an armchair in this elegant room while the Countess perched on the arm of my chair, and gave me directions about the farmers I was to go and see in the district. They gave me lots of cake and milk, and the two other women pumped me politely about my past, and told me I didn't look old enough to have been married two years! They knew various judges and people we know in Cairo, and that made me *quite* respectable. When I got up to go, the Countess asked me to come back for tea, but I didn't go, as I wanted to try and get home for the night. The boys pumped up the bike for me, and the Countess insisted on getting on to it herself, to see what it was like, although she's quite middle-aged. Then I went on my round of visits, mainly near Knebworth. I may be moving there next month, as it's a great potato-growing county, and they'll want gangs of women. There's a camp of German prisoners nearby, and they use a lot of them. The farmers say they work well.

Coming back, I got lost, and had two punctures and a breakdown and didn't get back till 9.30, as I had to push the wretched thing part of the way. But I didn't have to mend either of the punctures. One was mended by one of the farmers I'd been to see, and the other by a passer-by. I took it to the garage at Chesham, but even after that I couldn't get it home up the hill. But a very nice naval petty officer took command, and shoved it up the hill for me, and then put it right. Earlier in the day, a 'professional' type man pushed it up a hill. So I make use of all sorts and conditions of men. Mother says I'm a 'mollusc'; but why do things for yourself when a member of the opposite sex always seems to turn up handy, and be only too ready to do them for me? Today (Sunday) I've been doing things for myself, cleaning and polishing the bike. And Hugh helped me adjust the tuning, and explained things to me, so it ought to be all right. It really is a bit too heavy for me to push up hills. Yesterday there was a mule-cart in front of me, and when I sounded my horn, the mules started kicking in all directions. Their heels looked a bit too hard to meet me comfortably, so I put the bike between me and them. However nothing happened—except that I got some pretty awful language from the ASC men with the mules. I deserved it, for frightening them with my horn.

Chartridge
21.8.17

The sun's shining again at last. We put in an extra hour's work today, and finished weeding the wurzels. The farmer offered us the job of picking up the beans—which he tried to cart with the machine, but they were too battered down. My gang demurred—it's a horrid job—but in the end agreed, and so I'll be working with the same gang again. I'm keen to move on, and start a new gang somewhere fresh, but these would probably disintegrate, if I left them.

I'm supposed to get 3d a mile for my bike, and I've been diffident about putting in a claim so far, as I've been working from here—at Chartridge—and the distance to Tring is more than if I had a billet there, but of course, billeting at home costs me nothing. The B of A sent me another form, saying they'd not had my expense account yet, so I filled it in and sent it back, thinking they'd be bound to query my living so far from Tring. They paid the whole amount, but asked if I couldn't find a billet nearer my work, as this way it came a bit expensive. I felt rather a worm about it, so I've sent the cheque back, saying that I've thought it over and couldn't take money for travelling expenses when I'm living at home. There's little enough result to show for all I've cost in my training, and I'm getting such fun from my work and my experience with the bike, that I don't really want to be paid for it. Actually, it's the Herts Agricultural Committee that pays me, and not the Board. I hate them to imagine I'm 'on the make'.

One day I was sent to Stanmore, near Harrow, to see about placing a girl to work on the land for a large fashionable girls' boarding school. They were a bit alarmed to see me in my trousers. Then the Watford Labour Exchange sent me to various farms. It's the end of the forty days after St Swithin's day. The farmers say if it rains *that* day, it'll be wet for forty more. But it's fine today, so they seem satisfied. They're a superstitious lot, the farmers. One said the war was sure to end this year, as the beans were growing upside-down in the pods, and the last time they did that was the year the S. African war ended.

Chartridge
26.8.17

The weather is awful again, despite the farmers' prophecy. When it's too wet to work, I have to go all over the County on my bike, which gets choked up with mud, interviewing farmers, to persuade them either to have a Land Girl, or a gang of women, to replace their men. Mother thought I was overdoing things, and told Alice, who told Miss Kindersley, who has written to me to put in the weekly diary I have to keep exactly how many hours I work a day. I wrote back that was difficult. Fine days, I work six hours in the field, and visit farmers afterwards. And wet days I only visit farmers. Sometimes it takes two hours to interview one farmer. First, he has to be searched for throughout his meadows and farmyards, and then always talks for ages before I can get to the point. If he's nice, he takes me in and gives me tea, and shows me all over the farm. By the end of the time, we are pretty good friends and I've put my case fairly thoroughly for the employment of women, and have learnt all about him, and whether he's a suitable person to entrust a Land Girl to (some I soon realize *aren't*). It's really necessary to win the confidence of the farmer, and it takes time. But it's not work that can be assessed by the hour. It's really very pleasant dallying with interesting men, some nice, some not so nice. I'd be giving the B of A a false impression if I called it all 'work'. So I've written this to Miss Kindersley, and I hope she'll understand how platonic it all is, and that I won't be sacked for flirting with the farmers. Does it thrill you in the desert to be told of flooded roads and drenched garments which never seem to get dry? Of water running down all day between my coat and my

126

neck? Of my hair like rats' tails, and drowned rats in the ditches? That's life on the land—August, 1917! I went to see one farmer, near Tring, who has two hundred tons of damson plums to be picked next month, chiefly to be sent to seaports where they are used for fruit on ships, because they are little hard things that keep well.

Chartridge
30.8.17

Our bean-pulling is very depressing; we had one fine day when we worked for six hours. But before they could be carted, it rained again, and they are all mouldy and mildewed. Here are some of the remarks I heard my gang make today, when I was working very close to some of the women. They were talking of a girl in the village who'd had a baby. 'Is she married?' said Mrs L. 'No', said Mrs C. 'Bad luck for her then, and more trouble for her family', said Mrs L. 'Trouble, no fear', said Mrs C. 'She's a sensible girl. It's her master's child, and she's going back to service in the same place and leaving the child with her mother. He's sure to pay her well, and she'll make a tidy bit in the end. The insurance helped her over the bad time.' And again—'I saw Mrs B walking out with a fresh man last night', said Mrs R. 'She's a bad one', said Mrs C. 'She's always off with different men, no wonder her husband left her. I don't suppose he saw any fun in keeping four kids that weren't his. She should have done what I did—married the father of her children. Only with Mrs B, the men were all married already.' And Mrs A, speaking of her husband who's been missing for four months in France, said: 'It would be a rejoice if I could hear about him. But there, I always say if the children are all right one hasn't any real need to worry.' All the others agreed. The interest is in having children. Mrs A has had twelve and buried seven. Men are the medium through which they have the children, and marriage makes things more certain. Love between men and women, with these people, just doesn't exist. They aren't immoral, just *un*moral. In this village of about four hundred people, I should think at least three hundred and fifty think the way these women do. And it's pretty typical, though perhaps these canal villages are more primitive than others. It was almost the same at Barkway.

127

We've finished the beans, and I was planning to leave the district tomorrow. But the women begged me so hard to stay with them, and the farmer offered us the job of 'shocking' his corn (more useful than shocking the Ladies of Gezirah!), so I'm staying on.

Chartridge
5.9.17

It's trying work, shocking the corn. I was at it today from 9-6. You take a sheaf under each arm, and stand them up against each other, and then put five a side against them, like the roof of a house. It was barley, and all the beardy bits stick into you when you pick them up, And they got inside my smock, and my very thin breeches, so when I had a bath tonight, I came out in a rash, as if I had measles, and it was quite painful. My gang are really very sweet, though a bit crude. They know you're away, and that the mail is now so bad, so every day they say: 'We do hope and pray as how you may find your sweetheart at home when you get back tonight' And every day they ask if I've had a letter. One old woman of sixty-eight, whom we call 'granny', has a second husband with whom she doesn't get on. She says 'it's cos he's been a soldier and off to Egypt and them foreign parts, and that never does anyone any good—in fact, it spoils 'em downright.' I've at last finished with this gang, and I'm going back to Hatfield next week, to see what I can do round there.

Hatfield
10.9.17

I'm back at the Hatfield hostel, under the care of the old dame. I had a gruelling time getting here, as I went to see farmers of Harpenden and Wheathampstead and Hertford and other places on the way. Sixty miles in all — and I arrived long after dark, without lights. I really must get some, now autumn's coming on. Fortunately, no policemen about.

It's funny how I find out what farmers to visit. I was in the post office at Harpenden, and the telephone girl told me she had heard a certain farmer say over the 'phone that he wanted some Land Girls. So off I raced; he lives in a lovely sixteenth-century farmhouse, and wanted three trained Land

Girls to live in a cottage he had, and someone to look after them. I reported this to Hertford. Then I went to see a farmer at Wheathampstead whose two daughters, dressed as Land Girls, worked for him. His wife took a great fancy to me, and urged me to go and live with them, but I don't think she's all there! The husband has a name for being very bad-tempered and disagreeable—even thrashing his daughters—but he was very gallant with me, and I've risked his bad temper by placing two girls there as carters. He didn't want a gang, as he'd engaged a gypsy and his wife for the harvest. They live in a tiny tent made of a few hoops and a blanket stuffed inside with straw, which they wheel about in a push-cart, and pitch in the field where they're going to work. They are an interesting-looking pair. Then I went to see Lady Cavan again, and with her help, and that of the man at the post office, found billets for all the girls the various farmers wanted. Lady Cavan goes off to Paris next week to see her husband—lucky woman! She was very nice to me, and asked if I'd had lunch—it was then about 4. I said yes—though actually I'd forgotten all about it. She asked what I'd had, and when I said some milk the farmers had given me, she went and got me a meal herself in the dining-room, and made a most elaborate salad, and was extremely kind, but I felt rather like a tramp!

Today, the motor-bike broke down again, and I tinkered with it for an hour, and then I saw a wounded Canadian officer, in hospital blue, fishing nearby, and he came over and talked to me, and soon there were three very nice Canadian officers working on the bike, and they sat around while I ate my lunch. After another hour, they got it to go, and I went off to Redbourne. But then it broke down again, and a man came out of a house and took it into this yard, and for nearly two hours he and his assistant struggled with it, and at last it started, and I rode back to the hostel without more adventure. The man was a tanner, and a tanner's yard is not exactly the most pleasant place to wait in for two hours! It was so whiffy, and full of carcasses. These men who help all seem to enjoy it; they take command at once, and aren't at all interested in me, only in the bike. They aren't the sort I can give backsheesh to, of course. I don't suppose I'll ever really get stranded, as there always seem to be people to help.

The raids are getting quite bad, whenever there's a moon. In London, thousands of people go down the tubes every night, and have regular parties and picnics there. And people are leaving London for the country—I find it difficult getting billets for the Land Girls.

I've had to collect a gang for a farmer, to pick his damson plums, just over the border in Beds. It was difficult to collect them, and last Saturday evening I went back to London, still a few short. I wanted to take a taxi home from Kings Cross, and a woman came up and asked me to share one with her. She was interested in my uniform, and said she wanted to work on the land. So then and there I recruited her for my gang! This morning I went to see how she was getting on, and found her working away quite happily.

I'm staying here with Louie Pullar, the County Organizer, in her large house in a park, with heaps and heaps of books,. There are three guns at the end of the drive, and last night they were all firing, and the shells went whizzing over our house making no end of a row, and the shrapnel kept falling on the lawn; it was rather like seeing Tree's production of *Lear* at His Majesty's. It's difficult to realize there's someone up in the air, waiting to kill us. I'm much more conscious of the war when I'm hungry and try and get a meal somewhere, and am told 'owing to the war they've nothing to give me'. It happens nearly every day, and I mind that more than the raids. I had to go to the Faudel-Philips' place near here, and was looking very untidy. I saw the bailiff, and while he was showing me round, two regular Piccadilly men and two Bond St women appeared, and they (metaphorically) put up their monocles and lorgnettes and just stared at me. But I put on my most virtuous, religious expression, and pretended not to see them. I called on one old farmer who said he'd thank me to leave the women alone, and not come interfering. He had thirty women lifting his potatoes, and said they were such a trouble he often thought he'd pay anyone £1 a day to look after them. When I said I'd do it for less than £6 a week, he got very angry, and told me to go. I met one nice farmer who said: 'I was in the Dardanelles and it was good fun. I often sit and laugh over those times, and wish I were back again. I'd like to go to France in the summer—I don't mind anything except the cold. But they've sent me back from the Army to farm.'

Youngsbury
3.10.17

I've had a crazy adventure. I had a number of punctures in my back wheel, and couldn't get the last one mended till after 7. I tried to get hold of Miss Pullar to tell her I'd not come back for the night. She's not on the 'phone, and it was too late to send a telegram. I telephoned to the police at Ware, and asked if they could tell her, but they said a raid was expected, and they couldn't take any messages. So I thought I'd better try to get back. It was very misty, and about a couple of miles from the village where I wanted to leave the bike, and get to Ware by train, I lost my way. I saw some WD wagons and asked the soldiers the way. They told me my tyre was flat again, and said the bike was unrideable. They couldn't wait to mend it, but didn't like to leave me all alone on this very lonely road. So they put the bike in the lorry and I got into the cabin, and they took me to the nearest station. There I found there was no train for one and a half hours to Ware, and I'd have had three miles to walk to Youngsbury after midnight. So the soldiers said I'd better leave the bike at the station, and come with them to London, and they'd drop me at a tram or underground; they were going to Woolwich. The mist got thicker, and we had to deliver shells at some anti-aircraft stations, and they kept losing the way, and losing each other, so it was 11.30 by the time we reached the bus. I had to hide each time we came to an anti-aircraft station, as they weren't allowed to have passengers. I caught a bus from Wanstead to London Bridge. There a policeman told me, if I ran up the Borough High Street, I could just catch the last train at the Elephant for Paddington. I made a clatter with my Land Army boots on the pavement, and of course my motor-cycle kit makes me look like a boy. Some awful women were standing by a coffee-stall under a flare. They wore large feather-trimmed hats, and had blowsy painted faces. As I ran past they shouted: 'Stop, nice boy, stop. We want you to come with us.' I don't think I've been so scared in my life, and they ran after me all the way to the station, where I fell into the arms of the guard, who was just trying to shut the gates. To his surprise I gasped: 'They're after me.' So he told me it was all right, and I'd just be in time for the last train.

I got home safely in the end, and annoyed the household by waking them up at 1.30, because the door was bolted. I'd had no proper lunch, and nothing to eat since, so I was famished. Miss Pullar was out looking for me half the night, so all round I'm not very popular. But I don't see what else I could have done. There wasn't an air-raid, but when the police said they were expecting one, and the soldiers said the same, I was too funky to face the three-mile walk from Ware station with the shrapnel falling around. The soldiers were helpful and polite, and I was silly to be scared of those awful women. After all, what harm could they have done me? But it was all so weird at that hour of night, in the loneliness of the Borough High Street.

Chartridge
17.10.17

While the motor-bike is being thoroughly overhauled, I have to go everywhere on a push-bike. I did nearly forty miles yesterday, in the wind and the rain, and it was such an effort that it made my nose bleed some of the time. I had to see the girls in the plum-picking gang, because their farmer had been very unpleasant, abusive and rude, and refusing to pay them for the wet days, though he'd promised to do so. Eventually I found them another farmer to work for.

Wroxford
19.10.17

I am staying at Wroxford, near Hertford, with a family called Hogg. I find the daughters—now married—were at school with me. Mr Hogg is a great traveller and an ardent Tory. We sat up very late, arguing politics. I collected a potato gang for a farmer from the slums of Hertford. They are very bad slums, and a lot of the families are 'rag-pickers', and the rags are piled in the rooms where they live. I believe that the worst slums are in the towns around the large estates and model villages, because the families are turned out of the villages if a girl 'goes

132

wrong', and they gravitate to the worst parts of the towns. I said this once to a meeting where I had to speak at St Albans, and a nice old lady said: 'Ah!, my dear, you young people make such hard judgements, but you don't understand the problems.' And I found after she was the wife of the biggest local landlord, and very aristocratic.

As Hertfordshire was near London, and because of my contacts with 'Head Office', I was often asked to take part in recruiting campaigns and marches in the Metropolis. In 1917, I was asked to lead the contingent of Land Girls in the Lord Mayor's Show, as I wrote in my letter. Later, I went twice to Buckingham Palace, and made recruiting speeches in Hyde Park, Woolwich Common and various other places. I ought, perhaps, to have resented this favouritism, but at the time I took it all as a matter of course.

London
11.11.17

Whilst it's still fresh in my mind, I'll give you a full-length picture of the Lord Mayor's Show today. We assembled at the Drapers' Hall, in the City, at 9 am, all in our cleanest uniforms. There were a hundred Land Girls. We went into a lovely banqueting-hall, and had an enormous spread of meat rolls, coffee and marmalade, which was much appreciated by those girls who had travelled from a long way off. We were photographed, and then the past and present Masters of the Worshipful Company of Drapers talked to us about the origins of the Company, telling us they were connected with the wool trade, and not with the kind of drapers we knew in Oxford Street, and that confirmation of that could be found if we looked at the pictures of the women on the ceiling, and see how lacking in draperies they were. We were adopted by the Drapers' Company because either the Master or the Past Master has a granddaughter in the Land Army. Then we were lined up in the street, and it happened to be just outside Father's office, in Throgmorton Street. We walked up Cheapside to the GPO, where we lined up behind the band of the Grenadier Guards, with the Boy Scouts of the air-raid 'All Clear' units behind us. We waited there till noon, and crowds

133

came to look at us, and men threw us cigarettes out of office windows. I walked in front of all the girls, together with the instructors from Herts and Bucks, and our twelve Herts girls immediately behind. Many girls carried hoes, milk-stools, etc., and at the rear was a farm-wagon full of straw, with four girls leading the horses, and some sitting on the straw.

At last we marched off, by London Wall, Old Broad Street, Threadneedle Street, King William Street, Cannon Street, Ludgate Hill, Blackfriars, Fleet Street and the Strand, and we stopped in a little street leading to the Embankment, while the Lord Mayor went into the Law Courts to be sworn in. We disbanded and went to a Salvation Army hostel in Aldwych and had coffee and sandwiches. Then we lined up again, and marched up the Strand to Charing Cross, Trafalgar Square, Northumberland Avenue, all along the Embankment, Queen Victoria Street, and the Guildhall, from where we went back to the Drapers' Hall.

The crowd was lovely; they cheered us all the time, and there was no laughing or jeering, as we feared there might be, as girls in breeches are something new to the City. Officers in uniform, Tommies, wounded men in blue with their nurses, all clapped us as we passed. City men took their hats off, and waved them at us, and often called for three cheers for the Land Girls. And the children shouted: 'Hurray for the Land Women.' We had special ovations outside King's College and the City of London School. We certainly were a howling success, and were generally voted far superior to the Women's Army, who walked some way behind in khaki, and, it's said, didn't march nearly as well in step as we did. Our great help was the Grenadiers' band, and we found it inspiring to march to such martial music, although, till we got used to it, we were nearly deafened. There were two tanks in the procession, which looked ludicrously out of place in the narrow streets. And two captured aeroplanes, and some captured Turkish and German guns. There were also munition girls, women yellow from TNT, in wagons, and lots more scouts and cadets. But no soldiers except the bands.

A very nice old colonel took charge of us at the Guildhall, and marched us back to Throgmorton Street. He said he was proud to be seen with such girls. At the Drapers' Hall we had a big tea, and each of us was given an enormous box of chocolates. Miss Talbot, from the Board of Agriculture, was there, and spoke to us, and the Master Draper spoke again, and then we had a sing-song, and finally went home. I'll confess I enjoyed it enormously. It was all so good-humoured, and such fun being cheered.

Chartridge
12.11.17

We are all thrilled by what's happening in Palestine. It's wonderful that you're in the thick of it, working out the dream of your life. Balfour's manifesto gives the right touch to it all.

I've at last got my bike back, so life should be easier. I've been ordered to go up to Lincolnshire to do a job; I'm not looking forward to it at all.

Sleaford
21.11.17

I was annoyed when I was told I was to come up here without my motor-bike, and was determined to bring it. A sympathetic ticket-collector at Hatfield said that, if I had a Government warrant to say it was necessary to me for my war work, I could take it on the train. So I 'phoned Alice, at Head Office, and she nobly sent me a note at once to say I was going on official business. And I drained off the petrol, and before anyone had a chance to protest I shoved it into the guard's van, and here we both are. I hate being separated from it—it's bad enough being separated from my husband, let alone the bike too.

It's horribly cold here, and snowing. I biked the fourteen miles from Grantham; it's hideous country, flat and muddy, with no proper farms, only acres and acres of brussels sprouts. The landscape is dotted with telegraph poles, a few windmills, and the occasional church spire. Tonight I'm staying in a hotel; it's the first time I've stayed in a hotel alone. I don't know a soul here, and I feel rather miserable. But tomorrow I'll find a billet.

Sleaford
26.11.17

The farmer I'm working for is difficult. Every day he says he

135

won't have the gang working for him any more, and yet the next day he always sends for us. It's a vegetable farm, eight and a half miles away. About twenty women are collected every day from here in a motor char-a-banc, and I go on my motor-bike. The owner of the land round here is having two months in jail for potato profiteering, after having previously paid a fine of £4,000. After I've started the women working, picking sprouts, I go back to the town, to the Land Army committee rooms, and go around visiting other farmers for them. I've a nice warm billet. I was intrigued to see a large portrait of Thomas Hardy on the wall, and find my landlady is a relative of his. It's the dullest town I've ever been in.

I find it very hard to behave like a lady. I was walking in my Land Army kit through Sleaford today, when a man in mufti detached himself from two others and planted himself in front of me, saying: 'Well, kiddy, you're a real sport. I admire you from the bottom of my heart. I'm going back down under again next week and would like to shake hands with one of your sort before I go. Shake, girlie, and the best of luck to you.' So we shook hands. He went on: 'You're a marvel, kid. Why do you girls stick it? You're doing work we wouldn't give a bullock to do in Australia. I wish I could take you back there with me, girlie, you're one of the right sort. They don't appreciate you here. I've been saying this all around, and that's why I've got to quit. Deported, that's it, for interrupting Trade Union meetings, and telling them they shouldn't work for these damned wages. Stick up for yourselves, men and women. They've got you in their grip now, and they are moulding you, and when the war's over you'll be set and fast, and won't be able to rise. Now's your chance, girlie, fight for all you're worth. I know you're a lady, and I want to write to you, to tell you how we get on. I've been sent for today to Australia House, and the police are kicking me out of the country. So give me your name and address.' Here he produced a piece of paper and wrote on it 'Miss'. I told him I was married. 'You're more of a sport than ever', he said. 'Hats off to you.' I racked my brains for a fictitious name, but I was so muddled by his spate of talk, that I put down my real name and address. And he gave me his. 'Thank you, kid', he said. 'You're square. You'll write to me if I write to you. You're the first of your

136

sort I've talked to. Perhaps you think I shouldn't say all this, but in Australia we never let a chum down, and we never let a woman be put on. They're putting on you now, and that's why I want to help you. Good-bye, kid, and God bless you. You're a sport.

Then he went off, and left me breathless, and kicking myself for giving him my name and address. He's obviously some sort of agitator, and if my name and address are found on him, I may land in quod. I wish I didn't get so interested in people and anxious to know what comes next.

The gang was sacked yesterday, because only twelve turned up. They didn't mind; it was horribly cold picking the sprouts. I went to Swinehead to see if I could get another gang, but failed so I'll have to go ignominiously back to Herts.

I got into another queer situation, from being too friendly with strangers. When I went home for the weekend, I left my bike in a pub in Grantham. When I came back, Sunday night, I lost my way in the dark, trying to find the pub. A New Zealand soldier came up, and asked me what I was looking for, and seemed quite surprised when I said I was looking for the 'Barley Mow', as it's quite a little pub, in a slummy back-street. But he took me there, chatting happily all the way. I went into the pub, because I had to put on my biking overalls, while the landlady and various other people watched me with great interest. But the landlord was a brick. He got the bike out, and lit the lamps, and when it wouldn't start, he ran it up and down the road for me, to heat it up. When I asked him what I owed him for leaving it there for the night, he said, 'Nothing', and that he was always prepared to look after it for me. It was a very common little pub, but he was really nice. Today I ran out of petrol near another little pub, and the landlord took some out of a taxi he ran, and put it in my bike, so that I should not be stranded. And another man offered to sell me petrol coupons when mine gave out, but I'm afraid of that, as it's illegal. I feel more of a vagabond than a Land Army officer up here, and perhaps it's as well that I'm going back to Herts.

Food is getting as much of a problem as petrol. Often I can't get meals at pubs or tea-shops, as they say they've run out, and I get very hungry.

I feel absolutely wild at these new laws, taking the vote away from conscientious objectors. It's such a degrading thing for Parliament to do. What's the good of our fighting for freedom abroad and losing it at home?

East Barnet
30.11.17

I came back from Sleaford yesterday, as there was nothing else for me to do. I had rather a job getting my bike on to the train at Grantham. I hadn't a proper pass, and I just sat there in the station with it and refused to budge, until the officials got so bored with me, they finally pushed me and the bike on to a train going to Hatfield. But not before my lovely fur gloves had been stolen. Now I'm staying at the Rectory in East Barnet, with a pleasant clergyman and his wife, who are quite old, and very serious and religious—grace before meals, no meat on Fridays, and all that. Nothing light in the house to read; when I asked for something, they gave me the *Spectator* and the *Historical Geography of the Holy Land.* There's a funny little Siamese youth here, studying for Cambridge, and we're left alone together this evening, as the Rector and his wife have gone to church, as it's a Saint's Day. They got rather a shock when they found out I was Jewish.

I've signed on for 'National Service' for the duration of the war. I felt I had to do this, because I'm so tempted to chuck it all, and just work for the Labour Party, and yet I know it would be a mistake. So this is to ensure I don't do it in a moment of anger against all that the Government is doing. I don't want to make an ass of myself again, as I did in the Arsenal. People are beginning to talk of peace, because of Lansdowne's letter. If only it were true! The war gets more and more of a nightmare; and criticism and free thought are being stifled. I feel that the dislike of royalty and the bitterness of class against class has never been so bad as it is now. I hear so much as I travel around, and talk to all kinds of people in trains and eating-places. By the way, I have found out that my Australian friend at Sleaford was a member of some organization called the International Workers of the World. And he was deported for stirring up trouble in the camps. I do wish he hadn't my name and address on him.

138

Youngsbury
5.12.17

I'm here tonight staying with Miss Pullar, and having some lovely revolutionary talk. I was run in last night for riding without a light. But the policeman was a dear; it was freezing cold and very foggy, and I'd not been able to get any carbide, and when I told him this, and that I'd been out all day, and did so want to get back to my billet quickly for tea, he said: 'Well, get along. And if anyone else tries to stop you, pretend you don't hear. If you've no light they can't take your number.' He was really too nice to be a policeman.

Barkway
6.12.17

I've come back to Barkway, and have had a wonderful welcome from Mrs Whitby, my former billet-lady. It's no joke having lodgers these days, when food can only be got by begging and imploring the grocer to be kind to you. The farmer and his wife received me with open arms—and promises of unrationed petrol. It's all lovely, except for the mice running around the room, and the chilblains on my feet. I've also got toothache, but I cure this by smoking. I've been using a push-bike part of the time, because I'd run out of petrol. I did thirty miles on it today, and it helps to keep me warm. Actually, I'm always having trouble with the motor-bike when it's cold and damp. Next week I'm to make a speech in the village, because they are forming a new organization called a Women's Institute, and I'm to be a star turn, which rather alarms me.

1918—1919

The Land Army (2)

I had never been interested in acting, because one was required to repeat thoughts which had emanated from other people. But I had always had the ambition to be able to hold an audience by speaking my own thoughts, and being myself, not impersonating another character. This speech for the Women's Institute at Barkway, though unimportant in itself, proved both to myself and to those in authority over me, that I was capable of making speeches, and holding an audience. The war was dragging on endlessly, more and more men were needed, and they had to be replaced by women and girls. I wrote at the time how curious it seemed to see girls replacing men on the underground trains, and as drivers of cars. Recruiting campaigns for the various services were being held all over England, and in the early spring of 1918 it was decided to have intensive recruiting campaigns for the Land Army. It was then that I was in continual request as a speaker. My first meeting was on a market-day in Hertford, and I was extremely nervous—as I still am, whenever I have to make an important speech. And this speech was, to me, very important, as it would prove whether I were any real good at something I had longed to do well.

It was a fine, sunny day, and a hay-wagon was our platform. The Marquis of Salisbury presided, and Mr Barnard, an important man locally, was the next speaker. I stood with my foot on the wheel, ready to leap on to the wagon and start my speech as soon as he had finished. He was, I think, rather a dull speaker, and at one point, in order to show how good land-work was for those doing it, he touched my shoulder and said: 'Here's a fine specimen of healthy womanhood' but got no further. I leapt on to the wagon, and started off, in ringing tones: 'Women and girls of Hertford, the country needs you.' He sat down, amid roars of laughter, and I continued. When I finished, I was loudly cheered, and the District Organizer sent me a note: 'Magnificent! Get on your bike and race over to Hoddesdon, where there's a rally on, and repeat it there.' I felt successful, too, at my second effort. And then I became completely deflated. It was all so easy, and meant so little. Why had I wasted my ambition on something which anyone could do? On my way back to my billet, I left my motor-bike in a quiet lane, and lay under a hedge and wept and wept—something I very seldom did. Reaction, I imagine. But from that moment I abandoned ambitions. Life was so empty when one had achieved them!

I was sent all over the country, to speak at rallies, and was asked to speak at the biggest Land Army rally in Hyde Park one Saturday, and was photographed, and had my picture in the papers. At this rally a smartly-dressed elderly man came up to me and said: 'You're not speaking to the right people. Come and have dinner with me at Claridges tonight, and repeat that speech to the crowd of young women you'll find there.' To my everlasting regret, I refused. At the time it seemed too much like a 'stunt'. Later, I toured London in an open car, speaking in Oxford Street, Piccadilly, and wherever else I could collect a crowd.

I was chosen to be in the contingent of the Land Army which went to Buckingham Palace to be reviewed by Queen Mary. I was leading the front horse of a large wagon full of straw—it was actually a brewer's dray from East London, with its beautifully groomed horses. As we passed under Admiralty Arch, we were greeted by a group of naval officers. One of them shouted to us: 'Get up on it, lassie, it looks better that way.' So I, and the girl behind me, jumped on the backs of the horses. When we reached the Palace, we had to process round and round the courtyard, while Queen Mary watched us. It had recently rained, and the horses found it slippery on the wet paving. I hung on for grim life. When we stopped, the Queen came and spoke to me. She admired the horses, imagining they came from the country, and that I was the girl who looked after them. I hesitated to tell her

141

they came from East London, and that I normally had nothing to do with horses, but rode a motor-bike. Without actually telling lies, I let her believe that they were horses which I had under my personal charge, and which I had brought up to London that morning. When we left the Palace, I was besieged by reporters asking me to repeat my conversation with the Queen. We were filmed, and shown in the London cinemas.

On another occasion later on, when I was a Welfare Officer, we went again to Buckingham Palace, to be addressed by King George. It was a hot day, and some of the girls fainted. They were carried into the Palace, and others, wanting to see the inside of the Palace, started sham faints, till I went round, and threatened , in whispers, dire punishments.

But to return to my letters. I was sent to Essex for a time, to try and persuade farmers to employ Land Girls, in the attractive country, quite new to me, between the Crouch and the Black-water. From there I wrote:

Southminster
22.3.18

There never has been such a spring as this: the country is gay with fruit-blossom, hyacinths and daffodils. There are distant views of the sea over far-stretching marshes, and the water and sky merge in one great blue pattern. I can forget the war and the killing, until I get right down to the seashore, as I did today, and was stopped by a soldier with a fixed bayonet, forbidden to go further.

I have had to leave the motor-bike behind, as it was out of order again, and cycle everywhere on a push-bike. I went first to the office at Chelmsford, and then to Burnham-on-Crouch by train. I cycled to a fascinating village called Tillingham, and called on a farmer, late in the afternoon. He invited me in to tea, and, as his wife was out, I sat at the head of the table, and poured out the tea. He was an elderly man about sixty, with lots of children; while I was helping myself liberally to Devonshire cream and jam, in walked his wife, who was stuffy at seeing this intimate *tête-à-tête*.

I next went to the local registrar, who was supposed to find me a billet, but she wasn't helpful; so about 6.30 pm I decided to find one for myself. I cycled to Bradwell-juxta-Mare,

142

because I was fascinated by the name, and called at the 'Green Man', on the side of the quay. A disagreeable old man there said he couldn't have me ' 'cos there aren't no womenfolk about'. I went to another pub, where they couldn't take me, as they'd just had a baby, and there wasn't any room. I tried a number of cottages, but everywhere was told they hadn't any beds aired, and seemed to think it was heathenish when I suggested sleeping in them without. So I cycled to another village, and tried another local registrar, but she was unhelpful, and sent me across a lot of fields to the wife of their foreman, who said she 'couldn't think of it'. I think it was partly due to my kit, as they'd never seen a Land Girl before, and my breeches put them off. It was getting dark, and I felt miserable, and decided to sleep under a hedge. But it was cold, and a rat ran out nearby, so I went back to Bradwell, and happened to meet the village policeman. Fortunately, there was a full moon. He was a dear, and knocked up a lot more people, but they all refused. He said he'd take me home with him, but his daughter had measles, and he didn't like to suggest it. So he sent me to the Rectory, and the rector and his wife were perfectly charming, and I spent a very happy and comfortable night there. In the morning I went to family prayers, and the rector read the passage out of Matthew about the birds of the fields having their nests to go to, but the Son of Man having no place whereon to lay his head.

Today I came here, and have found a pub which seems all right. We can hear the incessant gun-fire. Everyone is feeling frightfully anxious, fearing the Germans are going to break through our lines.

Now it's tomorrow morning. The people at the inn refused to give me supper. They were as rude as could be—and there was a rat in my bedroom. I'm finding it more and more difficult to get meals. I've been to see the Food Controller here, because I can never get any meat, even with coupons. But he only said: 'My dear young lady, next time complain in writing. You certainly don't *look* starved.'

Sandridge
11.4.18

Yesterday I started a small gang at Rickmansworth, and today one in Harpenden. The weather is now horrible—snow and hail and incessant rain. The motor-bike is again out of order, but I'm staying here with a very nice family, and they've been driving me about in their car. They've told me something which rather shocks me. You'll remember I wrote about some Canadian officers who helped me with my bike, and with whom I afterwards ate my picnic by a river. They were dressed in blue, like wounded soldiers, but actually they were all suffering from VD. And I blush each time I think how I questioned them about being wounded!

It's getting easier to recruit gangs, now that things are so bad in France. Whereas last autumn they would say 'The pay's not good enough', now they say: 'We must turn out and help somehow.' Last week I was at Knebworth, and I'm starting a gang there on Monday. I put up notices all over the place beginning: 'Women of Knebworth, come and help with the 1918 crop'—and I spoke at a Mothers' Meeting and a Girls' Friendly Society Club, and I'm urging them to start a crèche to leave the babies while the mothers work. They already have a National Kitchen, where the elder children can have their dinners. Only the women say—and I can't help agreeing with them—'Why can't the *ladies* come and work on the land instead of us, and let us look after our own children?'

The local 'grande dame' was at one of my talks, very kind and condescending to me, rather in the way the English in Cairo talk to a promising young Egyptian. I was delighted when I found the one recruit I'd made for the Land Army was her cook!

Youngsbury

12.5.18

Friday night, when the motor-bike broke down, a very handsome chauffeur came and helped me put it right, for two hours, and then I took him to his home on my flapper-bracket. Yesterday I rode around the villages, seeing farmers, and the bike gave out again. It was a lonely part of the county, with many hills, and it was very hot. I pushed it four miles to Puckeridge, and went to a pub to ask for tea. The man said he couldn't give me any. I was completely whacked, so I said impetuously: 'If I give you my motor-bike, will you give me tea?' He agreed, and so I'll never see the wretched thing again.

I've been on a great recruiting stunt, all round London. I was in charge of seventy girls from Herts, and the procession was led by a fine-looking girl leading Hugh's beautiful collie dog, which caused a sensation. My job was to recruit all along the route. I ran by the side among the crowd, distributing pamphlets, and urging all likely girls to join the Land Army. I went into the big shops in Regent Street and Oxford Street, and talked to girls behind the counters and jumped on and off buses, and threw papers into the taxis. It's really all very childish, but while I was doing it, I got carried away, and could think of nothing except getting recruits. I ran into a girl I'd known in Cairo, in Regent Street, but she'd just married and wouldn't join. Then we went to Hyde Park, where I spoke from a wagon. Actually, we *did* recruit a number of girls. The only snag was my family were annoyed with me for doing it on a Saturday.

Don't you think it a great mistake to put Lord Milner in the War Office? One feels there must have been a lot of chicanery behind the scenes before he and Lloyd George could be united. I'm sure Labour won't like it.

Knebworth
21.5.18

I had a jolly Bank Holiday, with a big recruiting rally at Watford, and such a merry crowd cheering us all the time. I've bought another motor-bike, in Ware—a second-hand Hobart. It's more powerful than the last one, and shouldn't break down so often. On the other hand, it's heavier to push if it does. On the way back to Chartridge, I called in at Rickmansworth, where I've to find billets for twenty-five girls. A smart VAD came up to me, asking me to buy a flag. I said I would if she'd tell me where to billet my twenty-five girls. She immediately offered her stables, so I bought the flag. There's a spacious garage, chauffeur's quarters and a laundry, they'll do fine.

In the Harpenden area, I'm taking over the 'kennels', and arranging straw mattresses for the girls to sleep on. Six girls and their gang-leader are already there. One night, to try it out, I slept there alone, and found the mattress very uncomfortable,

145

as it had been filled tight with the straw, which was all wrong—it has to be loose. So I spent the night painting a big board with 'Land Army Hostel' on it in our colours, green and red, to put up outside. Next day, two friends arrived from the Hertford Office, and we re-made the mattresses.

So my letters went on full of my gangs, and the vagaries of the new motor-bike. Meanwhile, exciting things had been happening in Palestine. After being in the thick of the fighting with his camels as far as Jericho, Norman had been taken out of the Army to be Public Prosecutor in the Military Administration set up to administer Southern Palestine, which was in the hands of the British. At last his dream had come true: he was working in Palestine, in the work which was his profession, and for the British. He wrote very happily. And from then onward I was obsessed with the idea of joining him. I wrote to everyone who, I thought, might help me, but it was to be seven months more until we were united.

My billets alternated between the straw mattress on the floor and Sacombe House, near Ware, where I stayed with one of our voluntary workers, Aileen Hay, in the greatest luxury; between miserable little pubs and the comfort of staying with another voluntary worker, Laura Livingstone, in Bayford. (She was the sister of Sir Richard Livingstone, and of the wife of Dr Bell, Bishop of Chichester.) Occasionally, when I worked near Tring, I would impose myself again on Mrs Humphrey Ward.

I took part in one more recruiting rally, at my former workplace, Woolwich. Here I had to drive a brewer's dray, and having no head for heights, felt very nervous perched up aloft while the procession climbed from Beresford Square to the Common. I now had a colleague, Marjory McNair, who also had a motor-bike and would take over my work if I should suddenly leave. But the weeks went on, and it seemed that I would have to remain in England until the end of the war, so at the latter end of June I accepted the position of Welfare Officer to the Land Girls in Herts. This meant I no longer had to collect gangs—Marjory McNair took over this work; but I had to concentrate on finding billets for the growing number of Land Girls in the county, visit them in the evenings, settle their disputes with the farmers, and,

146

when there were enough in any one place, organize clubs for them.

The nursery-gardeners in Waltham, very near London, had turned over from growing flowers in their greenhouses to growing tomatoes, and needed a number of Land Girls. For some weeks I concentrated on looking after these girls. Most of them came from Yorkshire, a delightfully independent-minded lot of girls, not taking well to discipline (with which I sympathized). When I went to meet them at the station, the day they were expected to arrive, none were there. They turned up next morning, many of them wearing Australian soldiers' hats. They said they had never been to London before, and it seemed a pity just to change trains, and not have a look round. I rather failed in my welfaring; I asked no questions as to where they had spent the night. They were not happy at working in the overheated atmosphere of the greenhouses, as they had joined the Land Army hoping for a healthy life in the fresh air. Much of my time was occupied in smoothing things between them and their employers, and in organizing amusements for them in the evenings and on Sundays. Sixty of them were there, and whenever they felt annoyed, would go into the pubs, which was forbidden if they were in uniform. But, on the whole, they were delightful girls, and I could easily manage them.

On August Bank Holiday we invited thirty wounded soldiers to tea in a local hall, and organized a concert. First, we had a cricket match, and sports, to break down the usual constraint of these occasions. The concert was not a great success. Some friends from Hertford had offered to bring over a quartette. But the girls found this dull; so in a pause in the music, one jumped on the platform and said she was sure everyone was very grateful to the ladies, but it wasn't the sort of music they were used to. Then and there they broke into 'Roses of Picardy', in which all the soldiers joined, and until the soldiers left at 8 pm, one by one the girls came on to the platform and led off with all the popular songs. There was much kissing and cuddling when they said goodbye, and a return of the hats, which had been exchanged for the afternoon.

As Welfare Officer I had to attend meetings of the voluntary registrars, over which Miss Ward presided. These were held at the Kings Cross Hotel, as it was easier to travel from all parts of the county to London than to travel to Hertford.

In August I was given a fortnight's holiday, and again went to Ireland with Olive Franklin. I went in my land-kit—I had no other clothes fit to wear—and was called locally 'the girl with the man's legs'. Olive had short hair, and was called 'the girl with the man's head'. I enjoyed Ireland, though I was shocked at the poverty, the superstition and the lack of good education for the people. When I returned from leave I wrote:

London
16.9.18

Mrs Alfred Lyttleton is most interested in my wanting to come out to Palestine, so she asked Major Ormsby-Gore, a friend of hers, to see me. I went yesterday to the offices of the War Cabinet, (of course, in my farm-kit), and spent an hour with him. I'm afraid I didn't know how to leave, and he didn't seem to know how to get rid of me. He said he knew you, and he suggested I should go out as an organizer of women's land work in Palestine, and that I'd better take a party of about six other women, carefully picked. He said Mrs Eder, the wife of Dr Eder of the Zionist Commission, was anxious to go, and she could be one of them. I suggested your sister Nita, but he said on no account would Michael Lange be allowed to go, because of indiscreet things he'd said earlier in the war. Major Gore told me that Weizmann would be home in ten days, and I was to write a letter, stating all my qualifications, and what I wanted to do, and he'd talk it over with him. He'd talk it over also with Sir Mark Sykes, but warned me that, anyway, it would take time. Then he asked questions about the Land Army; his mother-in-law is Lady Salisbury, who is very good to the Land Girls, and he was quite interested. And he talked about you, and said you were doing a more useful job in the Administration than if you'd been on the Zionist Commission, as you had once hoped to be. And we went on to talk about Palestine generally—about the colonies, and the lack of religion among many of the Zionists, and their need to be tolerant to the fanatical sects found in the towns, and of the nationalization of the land. He was all for this, but I thought small-holdings better suited to the individualism of the Jewish

148

people. He said the Jews, and eastern people generally, never understood the keeping of stock, and that is where women from England, trained in this, could be of use. He was interested when I told him my Father was a member of the organization of British Jews, and anti-Zionist. He said this was a most un-British attitude, because England wanted the Jews in Palestine just as much for her own sake as for theirs. This intrigued me. And he said some harsh things about Lucien Wolf. It was all terribly interesting, and good of him to talk—and let me talk—for such a long time.

Knebworth
18.9.18

I'm here on a horrible job. One of the land girls here has died, and her family particularly asked that someone in Land Army kit should be at the funeral. As Welfare Officer, it's fallen to me.

We've now a caravan for a party of girls to live in while they tour the country helping farmers with the threshing. I started it off, and was to follow it up, but lost it at Welwyn. When I stopped an officer on a motor-bike to ask if he had seen it, he told me he had, some way off, and said I'd better hurry after it. I said I'd not enough petrol to go all that way, so he gave me a chit, and told me to go to a searchlight station nearby, where they gave me a whole can.

Hertford
15.10.18

Marjory McNair and I have taken a room here, with one bed between us, for eighteen shillings a week. It's all we could get; the people are horrid, they won't give us meals, or dry our clothes. But I've so much evening work, organizing the leisure-time of the girls, that I must be sure of somewhere I can sleep, if all else fails.

I went to London for another meeting at the Kings Cross Hotel, and in the evening to the Coliseum. After listening to masses of unfunny rubbish, I saw for the first time the Russian Ballet. It was my first experience, and I was enthralled by the colour and movement, different from anything I'd ever seen

149

before. Incidentally, I was 'on' in the cinema there for a whole week, when I rode the cart-horse to see the Queen.

Isn't the news marvellous? Actually, nobody here gets excited, which is a good thing, as I've always feared people would lose their heads when victory was near. But the peace-terms talk is still vague and inconclusive.

London
24.10.18

I'm up here, staying in digs in Ebury Street with Alice, for a Welfare Officers' Conference, held in Lord Astor's house in St James Square. The first morning we were addressed by Miss Talbot and Mrs Lyttleton, and then discussed. In the afternoon by Alice, on 'Labour' and 'Wages'; and next day on 'Women's Institutes', 'Rural Education', 'Girl Guides' and 'Libraries'. And in the evening the best talk of the lot on 'Welfare Work' by my old friend Miss Barker. And there are two more days of it. I'm feeling conceited, because Herts comes out well in welfare; but I know it's mainly due to Louie Pullar, Miss Ward, Laura Livingstone, Aileen Hay and the other voluntary workers. I don't at all like the woman who is the chief Land Army Welfare Officer. But she's all over me, because our county does so well, and because I've been taking a leading part in the discussions—actually, talking far too much!

The last night of the Conference was a dinner in a Soho restaurant, presided over by Miss Talbot. I had to reply to the toast of the 'Land Army'. I've no idea what I said—though I was told it was quite an impassioned speech—because, when I returned to Ebury Street, feeling very ill, I found I had a temperature of 104 degrees, and was in for an attack of Spanish influenza, then raging all over the world. Coming home from the dinner, near Victoria station, Alice and I heard a girl calling for help. We found her lying on the pavement, while a soldier was trying to lift her into a waiting taxi. When she saw us, she moaned: 'Don't let him. I don't want to go.' I rushed off for a policeman, and careered madly round the station, probably half delirious, yelling that a girl was being kidnapped. But no policeman was to be found, and when I returned to Alice, she

150

The Levis motorcycle near Tring, July 1917

Talking to the Queen, Buckingham Palace, March 1918

Helen and Norman Bentwich in Jerusalem

Norman on his way to the synagogue in
Old City

said she'd been unable to save the girl. This haunted me during my days of fever.

I was in bed in Ebury Street, a most unwelcome lodger, for eleven days, and my beloved Nana came to nurse me. When I was better, I still felt weak and depressed, and refused an invitation to walk for the second time in the Lord Mayor's Show. I saw Herbert Samuel about joining Norman in Palestine, and he told me to write again to Ormsby Gore. I went down to Youngsbury to stay with Louie Pullar, and as I was still too weak to travel round the country, I spent a few days working in a field, pulling up wurzels. It was while doing this that I heard the church bells ring, announcing that the Armistice had been signed. All the other workers rushed off home to 'rejoice', but I had a most depressing reaction, due, I suppose, to the 'flu. I lay under a hedge and wept and wept, and thought of all the suffering of the war, and of those who had been killed and maimed. And then I thought of the future, and what a terrible mess there was to be cleared up, and how the better Britain we had fought for seemed as far off as ever, and, for the first time, I realized the futility of the war, and asked myself why I'd been believing it was the right thing all these years. When I went in to lunch, Louie asked me to go up to London with her, to see people celebrating the end of the war. But I refused: there seemed so little cause for celebration, as if the real struggle was still to come. I spent the afternoon sitting by the fire, reading Edward Carpenter's poems, which Louie had recently given me.

But I soon recovered, and went to stay in my old billet at Barkway again for a time. Norman wrote that he was now Senior Judicial Officer in the Administration, and the day of our reunion was the only thing we were both living for. But it was still some way off, and I continued with my letters.

London
22.11.18

I've had a busy week. At the week-end I had to be in the Watford area, and I stayed with Lord and Lady Clarendon in their lovely house near there. I had some entertaining talk with Lord Clarendon, giving him my views on the Labour Party, explaining (!) Guild Socialism, and telling him what it feels like to be a bullied factory hand. In return, he told me about agriculture in Canada, and big game shooting. On Sunday evening I came down to dinner before the family, in my Land-Army kit (my only clothes these days), and found two very conventional, very tall Guards officers, in mess kit, in the drawing-room. They stared at me blankly for a while, and then tactfully started talking of the crops. The situation in Palestine came up for discussion during dinner, and they made some derogatory remarks about Jews. Lord Clarendon hastily turned the conversation; he knew I was Jewish, because I had had to tell him why I couldn't accompany them to the special Armistice service in the church that morning. I could, of course, have gone, but when they knew I was Jewish, they took it for granted I wouldn't want to.

London
29.11.18

Last night I went to a ball at the Albert Hall, and danced weird dances with American navy boys, and various others. It was American Thanksgiving Day, and they had a naval party, and invited WAACs and WRENs and Land Army Girls to dance with them. Marjory McNair and I were the only real articles, because other girls were too busy working. But all the Head Office staff (including Miss Talbot and Alice) dressed up in Land Army uniform and came along. We had a special box, and we helped sell things for St Dunstans. We made glad eyes at US sailors till they asked us to dance, which I did very badly, putting it down to farm work not being conducive to good dancing. One—an officer—said: 'Say, little Land Army Girl, you're real her*oi*nes', pronouncing it like a 'y'. He and I hit it off well, he being a combination of lawyer and farmer. But when we came to our third dance together, a lady friend of his came and pulled him away from me, although he said: 'Little Land Army Girl, I want awfully to dance with you again.' His lady-friend looked 'through' me, as if I didn't exist, the way some people look at servants. But I enjoyed the evening, and didn't get home till 1.30 am.

Hatfield
9.12.18

I nearly came to an untimely end in Hoddesdon on Tuesday. In passing between two carts on my motor-bike, a cow ran into my front wheel and sent it spinning round, and into the front horse of one of the carts. The horse gallantly saved my life by stepping on to the pavement instead of on to me. All Hoddesdon ran out screaming, because they thought I was dead. But nothing worse than a buckled front wheel.

The election campaign is in full swing. One evening Louie and I raced around, putting 'Labour Manifesto' tracts into the letter boxes of all the most Tory people in the neighbourhood who should read them, for the good of their souls. And I had a thrilling time one night. I went to the big Labour meeting at the Albert Hall with Louie, and helped her to steward—although it's strictly against regulations, as I'm an 'official of the Board of Agriculture'. The hall was packed, and over two thousand people were outside, unable to get in. A large number of professional men and women and crowds of manual workers, and many older men and women, followers of William Morris, to whom this meeting seemed the culmination of all they had striven for. First, the Red Flag was sung, and other Labour songs. Adamson, the leader of the Labour Party in the House, spoke first. He kept alluding to the 'great and glorious victory', and he was howled down, the audience sang the Red Flag again. They yelled 'Are we Bolsheviks?' and some answered yes, and some no. And they shouted 'Where is John Maclean?'—he's the man who got five years for inciting the Clyde workers. Lansbury rose and appealed for the right of free speech, and then Margaret Bondfield, who told them they weren't fit to run a tripe shop, let alone a nation. Thomas, of the Railway Union, spoke next, and Smilie, and Henderson and Mary McArthur; Henderson was the best. They were all dead against a bloody revolution, and Lansbury said it's as bad to kill a capitalist as a German, and we must learn to *love* and not to *hate*.

I long to throw up the Land Army and work for Labour in the election. There are four hundred Labour candidates. I'm hardly on speaking terms with Father, he was so appalled at my stewarding at the meeting. To him, all Labour politicians are Bolshevik. But he only reads *The Times*, which gave the impression that all the speakers at the meeting were inciting the workers to revolution, when it was just the reverse. Some people say Labour is wrong to leave the Coalition. I believe they must.

The result of the election was a foregone conclusion, and the Coalition won easily. From my restricted angle, I saw the whole campaign as dominated by the two blusterers, Pemberton Billing and Bottomly, and I was disgusted. There was no idealism, no real thinking, just an emotional orgy of 'Hang the Kaiser', and 'Make the Germans pay.' It made me feel even more stupid at having, for so long, believed in the 'ideals' for which we were fighting.

My life was now divided between organizing Christmas parties and entertainments for the Land Army Girls—even writing sketches for them to act—and waiting for hours, among milling crowds, at the Passport Office. I had at last received permission to go to Palestine, not just to join Norman, because the shipping shortage made it impossible to allow all the wives who wanted to go, to join their husbands, but on condition that I undertook to do social work there. One day, I was shown into the private room of a very friendly official, who at last gave me my passport. As I entered the room, an elderly bearded Jew left it. 'What has a girl like you in common with a man like that?' I was asked. 'Isn't it better for you to stay here, rather than join him in Palestine?' 'We have much in common', I replied. 'We are both Jews': and he said no more.

Alice told me later that there was a threat to withhold my permit to go to Palestine, because a report from the Arsenal was in my 'file', and alluded to my 'Bolshevik tendencies'. However, this was overcome, due, I have always believed, to the intervention of Mrs Lyttleton.

The last visit I paid as a Welfare Officer was to the north of the county. There was some trouble between Land Girls and a farmer, and I was to visit the girls, and spend the night in the cottage where they were billeted. It was a dark, wet evening, and my motor-cycle broke down some four miles from my destination. A man came out of a nearby cottage and tried to put it right for me. But eventually I had to abandon it, and pushed it into his shed. I set out to walk the rest of the way, but had not gone far before the man appeared and said he would walk with me, and on we trudged. When I saw the lights of the cottage I was to go to away on a hill, I thanked him, and said he need come no farther. He then put his arms round me, and tried to kiss me. I was so horrified that I hit him—hard. He fell backwards into a ditch, and I found myself using language I had never thought of since I left the Arsenal. He lay there, in the mud, looking completely ridiculous as he touched his forehead and said 'Sorry, I didn't realize you was a lady', and I ran as hard as I could up the hill to the waiting Land Girls. Marjory McNair fetched the bicycle some time later, after I had left the country, and bought it from me.

I sailed from Liverpool early in January. My last days in London were spent hectically buying clothes. I was unable to stay at home, as the whole household, except Mother and Nana, had the virulent influenza. Hugh's wife, Elsie, died the day before I left, and he and Ellis were both dangerously ill when I departed. I tried to postpone my departure, because, having had the illness already myself, I could have helped with the nursing. But I was told I must go on this ship, or wait probably several months for another. It was an Orient liner, carrying Australian soldiers home, and only a very few civilians. When I arrived at Port Said, Norman met me in the privacy of my cabin with a cable saying my brothers were recovering. After a few days in Cairo, we travelled to Jerusalem to begin a new life together.

1919—1920

Jerusalem

The journey from Egypt to Palestine was now made by train. We left Cairo at six in the evening, and at Kantara crossed the bridge over the Suez Canal in an army wagon, to catch the Palestine train, arriving at Ludd at six in the morning, to continue the journey to Jerusalem by car. We had to wait nearly three hours for Norman's official car, as it had broken down on the way. But I was told that was what one had to expect of cars here; they were mainly 'Tin Lizzie' Fords, and anything but new. And the roads were appalling. We stayed at the same hotel as we had before, now taken over by the Army and Navy Board for the use of officers and their wives. I was only the fifth wife to arrive, the other four having joined their husbands from Egypt. We paid seven shillings a day—all our meals included.

On 26 January I wrote to my mother:

Here I am in Jerusalem, and such a Jerusalem as we could never have imagined when we were here five years ago. Cars and lorries racing through the streets, clean and well-ordered bazaars inside the old city, law and order everywhere, and free access to the Dome of the Rock and the Holy Sepulchre, both of which I have visited as easily as going into Westminster Abbey. Today I went to see Miss Landau, at the Evelina de Rothschild school. I sat with her for two hours while she talked, and gained much useful information. In particular I learnt that there is an immediate need for work for the many

156

unemployed Jewish girls who are, some of them, becoming 'camp followers'.

I then went to the offices of the Zionist Commission. Dr Eder, who is the head of it here, is away in London, and all I obtained from the bearded man I eventually saw was that I must learn Hebrew first, before I could undertake any social work. Knowing my incapacity for learning languages, I told him that the girls would all be grandmothers before that was achieved, and that I believed that the lives of these girls were of more importance than any language, adding that I had only been allowed to come to Palestine on the undertaking that I would do social work, and that I intended to do whatever I could immediately. I can see that life will not be easy here!

Within a few days of my arrival, I had collected together some of the girls who were considered to be in moral danger, and had persuaded the owner of a large neglected garden on the Jaffa road to allow me to use it for growing vegetables. I was fortunate in finding a capable and devoted woman instructor, who had been trained at the farm-school at Kinereth, which we had visited in 1914. Ten girls had started digging and hoeing by the time I wrote my next letter home. They worked for six hours a day, six days a week, and I paid them two pounds a month. I had hopes of selling the vegetables later at a profit. The girls were enthusiastic, and soon I was able to obtain the use of a large tract of land behind Jerusalem's only cinema (which is still there). I borrowed tools from the Army, and begged seeds and plants from various sources. I decided to try growing potatoes, which in those days had seldom been grown in the Judaean hills, and were almost prohibitively expensive to buy in the market. The Quartermaster in charge of the stores allowed me to visit his potato store, and to choose those with the most 'eyes' to use as seed. The results were successful, and later in the year our new potatoes were welcomed as an unusual luxury by the English housewives.

Land-work was the only thing I knew much about, and I hoped that some of the girls would later take up work in the Jewish villages and settlements. Every morning I visited the gardens, to see how the work progressed: at first, I had to walk, as I had no means of transport. But later, we acquired a white Arab horse, and I would ride round the town, followed by Norman's 'sais' (groom) on his bay. One morning, as I was passing through some olive groves, a bullet swished by, narrowly missing my head. This scared me, but when I told the authorities, they just advised me to ride a different way each day. They thought, though, that it was probably an accident, and not an attempt at assassination.

How to find the money to support this small, amateur venture was always a problem. Fortunately, I had saved most of the money I had earned during the war, and my mother collected money for me in England. I gradually acquired more land, and later employed over sixty girls; Norman was generous in allowing me to use his savings, too. Although I sold most of the produce, the gardens were never self-supporting.

We soon found a small house in the German Colony, a well laid out suburb to the south of the town, with pleasant gardens and many trees. In about 1870 a number of Germans from South Germany had migrated to Palestine, to live a more Christian and pacifist life than they had felt to be possible under the increasing militarism of Germany at that time. They had formed small colonies in Jerusalem, Jaffa and Haifa, where they engaged in skilled trades, and in agriculture. They were known as the 'Templars'. When the German Emperor, Kaiser William, came to Palestine in 1899, he reclaimed their loyalty as patriotic Germans, and thereafter some of them were agents of German influence. During the Sinai campaign, one of them was an active German spy, and was discovered, dressed in British uniform. After the occupation, most of the men, and certain of the families, were interned in Egypt, and their houses were taken over by the military.

Our house had nine rooms, and a loggia, but no bathroom. I went to the store where the German furniture was kept, to select what I needed. Later, during the hot weather, some of this furniture produced an unpleasant outbreak of bugs.

We moved into the house with the help of convicts; officers were allowed to use them, without payment, and we continued to use them for heavy work. One day, they burst into my sitting-room, where I was having tea with some friends, in great distress, because their guard had not come to fetch them, and they were afraid they might be locked out for the night. There seemed no stigma attached to being in prison, and they were a common sight marching through the town in their blue and white

158

cotton clothes. Later, some British officer insisted on fastening chains from their waists to their ankles, and after that I could not bear to employ them.

Jerusalem is a city of violent changes of climate. It stands nearly three thousand feet high, and in the winter it can be extremely cold, with biting winds, fierce rainstorms, and occasionally snow. The winter of 1919 was exceptionally cold, and at first we had no heating of any kind. But after a few weeks, the Quartermaster General came to dine. Hearing we had no heating, he brought his own oil stove, and we persuaded him to leave it behind.

My letters home continued. In February I wrote:

We are now well settled in our house, with a Jewish housekeeper and housemaid, and Norman's Sudanese batman. We live almost entirely on Army rations. We've borrowed beds from the American Red Cross, who have a unit here. I've already become involved in a committee of Jewish women, where all the talk is in German. I am amazed at the chaos in their social work activities, and immediately proposed a plan to divide Jerusalem into districts, each with its allotted social worker, to keep efficient records, and to work with the family as a unit. To my surprise, my plan was accepted—'in principle'. That's a wonderful phrase, which I'm discovering means that no immediate action should be taken, and so all my ideas are put into cold storage.

Norman is chairman of the orphan committee, to look after Jewish orphans—'orphans' include all children whose parents are not able to bring up their children properly, and there are thousands of them. Already, 'children's villages' are being established in different parts of the country.

We have been to tea at the Headquarters of the Administration, in the German Hospice on the Mount of Olives. This is a pretentious building, with a marvellous view from its high tower. It had been planned by the Kaiser when he was here, in 1899, and the roof of the chapel has a representation, in bright mosaics, of the Kaiser and his wife, holding a replica of the building, presenting it, I presume, to God. General Money, the Chief Administrator, is away, and Ronald Storrs, the Governor of Jerusalem, was acting in his place. English women are a

159

rarity here, and many nights a week we dine in the various messes.

Storrs played a large part in the life of Jerusalem in the early days of the Mandate, and was always a controversial figure. He was a brilliant and stimulating talker, and no occasion when he was present was ever dull. A great lover of music, he played the piano well, and together with Norman, who played the violin, would entertain his guests in the large room of his house in the town, which was full of exquisite hangings and pottery, and shelves of the latest books, which he was generous in lending to his friends. He had previously been the Oriental Secretary in the British Residency in Cairo, and had brought his possessions up from there. Ernest Richmond, the son of the artist, was living with him at that time, another controversial figure, intensely pro-Arab, and later, when he became political secretary, a bitter anti-Zionist—as were some other officers in the Administration. The English society of my early days in Jerusalem was small and closely-knit, and we met each other almost daily.

But from the first, we decided to do all we could to make our home a meeting-place of people from all the various communities of Jerusalem and to try to make the society different from that we had found in Cairo. And Storrs, too, set out to do the same. We gave frequent lunch and dinner parties, and always had a mixture of British and local guests. Later, there were various foreign consuls to be included, and a growing number of tourists. My letters continue:

We went to tea at a large orphanage here, originally run by a German, Pastor Schneller, and now by the American Red Cross. They have a system of law courts, run by the children, which they wanted Norman to see. It was all very well done—four boy judges and one girl, who was blind. They were all Arab children—very intelligent and realistic in their 'sentences'. It was impressive to see how quickly these Arab children responded to modern ideas of self-government.

The Arabs and Jews *don't* love each other—I'm sure the folk at home who talk so glibly of the Arab and the Jew lying down side by side like the lion and the lamb don't know much of the real feeling here. It's very deep—and the Jews are not as

160

tactful as they might be, in trying to make things easier. If only we had some really strong Jew here, apart from the Administration. Those Jews who are inside the Administration, like Norman, can't really help. I think Jews in England don't realize what chaos and muddle there is among the Zionists—too many dreamers and too few do-ers. One of the great changes since 1914 is that Moslem and Christian Arabs are now united, and have set up a combined organization against the Zionists. But it's no good my worrying too much over the vagaries and peccadilloes of the Zionist Commission and the Jewish community here—I'm completely impotent to do anything about it. The one strong man in the Zionist Commission is a very intelligent Italian, Commandante Biancini, with a most picturesque way of talking English. [He was later murdered in a train, near Damascus.]

We've had lots of parties, with some very interesting people. One guest was Father Waggett, a delightful man in the Intelligence at HQ, here to advise on religious affairs. And Major Sackville-West, who travels all over the country in a carriage, collecting the Ottoman debt. And Dr Glazebrook, the American Consul, from Virginia, a charming old man who fought, when very young, in the American Civil War. Mr Ashbee [C. R. Ashbee of the Arts and Crafts Movement], who has been brought here by Storrs to revive the native handicrafts and advise on the planning of Jerusalem, is one of the very few Britishers not in uniform. I see a lot of him, and we have great political talks. He wanted my garden-girls to make flower-gardens all round the Jaffa Gate—but the Arabs objected to Jewish girls doing this.

During 1919, although the political situation was perpetually volcanic, there were no outbreaks of violence. But below the surface the atmosphere was tense and unhappy. Most of the British officers in the Administration were declaring themselves openly opposed to the Balfour Declaration, and, as I had written home, the members of the Zionist Commission were not always tactful in dealing with those in authority. As there was no official censorship I wrote home very freely about the conditions, and this led to an incident which disturbed me. I was told by one of Norman's colleagues that a 'Secret and Confidential' document was being circulated among the higher officers of the Administration compiled by one of its members who was known as a virulent anti-semite. This document was directed against the policy of the Balfour Declaration, and in particular condemned the Zionist Commission. In it the writer stated that he was not alone in criticizing that body, as the wife of a highly-placed British Officer, who was a Jew, was indulging in similar criticisms in letters she was writing to her mother. He proceeded to quote passages from my letters, with complete accuracy, as I discovered when eventually I managed to see a copy of the document. I resented this deeply: there was something unpleasantly treacherous in a British officer opening in secret letters written by the wife of one of his colleagues, at a time when there was no censorship, and using the contents for political purposes. Of course, I was less outspoken in my letters home in the future. But this incident made me feel ill at ease with a number of men whom I had formerly accepted as friends, and I became less happy and carefree in the life I was leading. I was being drawn into the vortex of Palestine politics, and I realized that no man or woman who was Jewish could escape involvement.

But there were always excursions into the country, and our regular week-end picnics; I wrote home a full account of one of the tours, as well as one of the more sensational picnics.

We left home at 5.30 am in a box-Ford car, with an English driver who came from Italy a fortnight ago, and had never driven anything but lorries before. A few miles north of Ludd, a wheel came off, and was fixed on temporarily, till we found a Motor Transport Depot, and called in for help. There were no spare wheels, only a number of odd parts, and it took two and a half hours to repair. Meanwhile, we walked into the Officers' Mess, to find them all in a condition of complete 'negligé'. They were horrified at seeing a woman, and all bolted to return shortly well-shaved and properly clad. After travelling a few more miles, a tyre burst, and had to be reparied. We drove over the Plain of Sharon—no roads, only tracks, and we got lost a few times. Soon another tyre burst, and the sun was fierce, and there was no shade. After eight hours, we reached Tal Keram, and had a meal with the District Governor. We

162

drove on to Zichron-Jacob, and spent the night with Norman's sister. Next, to Haifa, where I had a welcome swim. After lunch, we went in a touring Ford to Acre—*we* should have had this car all the time, but one of Norman's staff had taken it, and Norman never makes a fuss. Acre is lovely—and it was a gorgeous drive, all along the beach, generally with one wheel in the sea, and Arabs posted to warn us of quick sands—quite a lot of cars had been lost in them. We weren't allowed to go much round the town, as the night before there had been a fight between Tommies and Arabs, and the two Arabs killed were being buried. In the evening, we dined with the Governor of Haifa, and stayed in a German convent. We were to have stayed with one of Norman's English officers, but his wife had eloped the day before, and he was too upset to have us. Next day, we went to Nazareth, and stayed the night, and visited Mrs Romilly, the wife of the Governor (who was ill). She's a sister of Winston Churchill's wife. Then along roads and tracks to Jenin and Nablus—we stuck in the sand for an hour at one place, till we could push the car out. The roads are covered with huge stones, so we had to drive on the tracks. They are waiting for a steam-roller—the story goes that there are only two in the country, and they collided near Bethelehem, and a new one has to be found. We lunched with the Governor of Nablus, and started off, when the back tyre burst, and the driver sat on the running board and cried. So we walked back to Nablus, and stayed the night, while the car was repaired.

And later I wrote of a trip on Easter Sunday:

Norman, Judge Corrie and I went riding to the Monastery of Mar Saba, which lies in the Judaean hills, towards the Dead Sea, and is said to be the place where Holman Hunt stayed when he painted *The Scapegoat.* It belongs to the Greek Church, and no women are allowed to enter. I sat outside, and a cushion was brought for me to sit on, and a bunch of flowers, and some coffee. In some places, the track is steep and stony, and on our return journey Norman's horse slipped, and he went head over heels and cut his face badly. A Bedouin family suddenly appeared out of the blue—they must have been watching us from the hills—and the woman brought water in a

163

pottery jar, and helped me wipe away the blood, and the man led Norman's horse back to the Monastery. There the monks washed the wound with Arak, which they said was a good disinfectant. When we got home, he had an anti-tetanus injection, which gave him a fever, and a nasty rash.

My domestic affairs, after a time, were a problem. The Jewish cook found our constant parties too much work, and eventually we found an excellent Berberine, from Egypt. But even he was a problem on one occasion. The day before we were to have General Money—the Chief Administrator—and Lady Money to lunch the cook disappeared. Panic-stricken, I begged the police to find him, which they did, in a lock-up a few miles from Jerusalem. However, they kindly let him out for the day, to cook the lunch, on condition he returned immediately after, which he did. Fortunately, he only received a short sentence.

In the spring, I went to Cairo, to arrange about bringing up all the furniture from our flat there. Cairo was full of rows and troubles, and travelling was quite difficult. I stayed for a few days with old friends there, and in the end arrived back safely. I wrote home about some of our entertaining, and Jerusalem parties:

Judge Brandeis, a judge of the Supreme Court in America, is here, and dined with us. He has come for a short visit in connection with the Zionist Commission. He is a most attractive person. He listens a lot, but says little, which is the wisest thing here, where the most trivial remarks uttered by an important person are quoted and mis-quoted, and shouted from the house-tops, as well as being used as propaganda by all sides. He listened attentively to all that Norman told him. He had with him Alfred Zimmern, an Englishman, half-Jewish, who is also a charming person. He writes and lectures on international affairs . . .

We have been to an evening party at the Grand New Hotel, inside the Old City (it's neither Grand nor New!) All the Jerusalem notables were there, including the Mufti, whom I like very much. [This was the predecessor of the notorious Haj Amin.] The non-Moslems brought their wives, and there were a number of British officers. For two whole hours we sat, without changing places, on hard chairs placed right against the walls. Occasionally a callow young Armenian played the violin, and a nervous British Tommy sang sentimental songs. Tea and masses of sticky cakes were brought round to us, and then our host gave a lengthy oration in Arabic, later translated into English, saying how much better the world was for gatherings of this kind where people of different nationalities met in such a happy atmosphere, and how much we really all loved each other. (He is a Bahai, on Norman's staff. They are a Persian sect believing in brotherly love. The party was in our honour.) Considering that the leaders of the most anti-Jewish section of the Arabs were there, and some of the most ultra-chauvinistic Zionists, it seemed something of an exaggeration . . .

Miss Landau has given an enormous and successful fancy-dress ball, which was nearly ruined by one of Jerusalem's everlasting 'incidents'. The night before there was a concert in the cinema to mark the opening of a music school. In the front row were the senior British officers, including General Money. Miss Landau was sitting with them. At the end, the performers struck up what they thought would be 'God Save the King', so they all stood up. But it turned out to be the Zionist national anthem, so they all sat down, including Miss Landau, who is known to be anti-Zionist. So a number of the Jewish people said they would boycott Miss Landau's party, and next day Jerusalem was buzzing with this 'incident', and poor Norman was asked to go and call on one after the other, and persuade them to come to the ball. He was quite successful, and most of them came.

The third party was one I gave, on the occasion of a conference in Jerusalem of all Norman's law officers from the whole country. It was given in the Law Courts, part of the large and impressive compound built by the Russians for their pilgrims. It was a bleak building in which to have a party, but I decorated it with all my own—and borrowed—hangings and cushions, and petrol-tins of shrubs and flowers, and it was quite attractive. Everyone who was anybody in the town was invited—about three hundred came—and I rallied all my friends to cut sandwiches and make lemonade and cakes. The problem was that, being official, we had to have one special part for women, as we'd invited the Moslems to bring their wives. Unfortunately, not many came. But I arranged that *all* the women, of whatever religion, should stay in the reserved rooms until Lady Money had come, and spoken to any Moslem women who were there, and then all who wanted to could mix with the men. It worked quite well. My real difficulty was in keeping my guests 'circulating', instead of sitting in rows on chairs, as they usually did at local parties.

All this time, I continued my work with the 'land girls'. I'd been asked to join the 'Jerusalem Council of Social Service', of which Mrs MacInnes, the wife of the Anglican Bishop, was the chairman. We soon were able to start a rescue home, with an English woman from Cairo in charge. And, after a hard battle, and staunchly supported by Ronald Storrs, we had all the brothels shut down in Jerusalem, much to the annoyance of the army.

So life went on—gay and interesting on the surface, but full of ill-feeling and insoluble problems underneath. We acquired a 'Tin Lizzie' Ford, and I was taught to drive it, by a British sergeant, on the Jericho road. I was the first woman to drive a car in Palestine. But I still kept my horse, and rode it daily to visit the girls. One day, in December, I was riding through the town, when a messenger from the Law Courts came running after me, to say I was wanted at once by my husband. He had heard that we were to leave that night for Egypt, to catch a troopship to go home on leave. Somehow, with the help of many friends, we got packed, and left our house in fit condition for a temporary tenant. Norman had not been home for over four years, and badly needed leave. He was suffering frequently from dysentery.

The journey home, to Liverpool, took a very long time, as the crew went on strike on Christmas Day, when we were off Gibraltar. The waiters walked out in the middle of our Christmas Dinner. Norman was the senior-ranking officer, so to entertain the company he played his violin. In the end, the waiters returned to give us our Christmas pudding, but refused to enter the dining saloon till 'that awful noise had stopped'. Poor Norman, he was really rather a good violinist!

We returned at the end of April, 1920, to be met at Port Said by the news that there had been serious rioting in Jerusalem. On 30 April I wrote home:

166

Sir Herbert Samuel with Lord Balfour and General Allenby in Jerusalem

Sir Herbert Samuel as High Commissioner

We've arrived in Jerusalem to find no end of intrigue and clamour about the row on Easter Sunday. Inquiries and commissions and court martials without end. Officers in the Administration have got the wind up, and keep asking Norman what people are thinking at home. Mostly, they care more for their own positions than for the future of the country. At the moment, Norman is much in demand everywhere, as they all want him to hear *their* side of the story. It's undignified of the British to get the wind up in this way. The whole position, between Arabs and Jews, seems just like Ireland. Most of the British treat the Jews as the offenders because, as one simple-minded staff captain told me: 'The Jews are so clever, and the Arabs are so stupid and childish, it seems only sporting to be for the Arabs.'

It's rumoured that the French are behind the Arabs. The British here are always convinced that the French are our allies, it seems, and the Germans still our enemies. They continue to turn the Germans out of their homes, and requisition their houses for themselves.

A few days later, we learnt with pleasure and excitement that the military government was coming to an end, and that a civilian High Commissioner was being appointed. Our joy was great when we heard it was to be my uncle, Herbert Samuel. When he arrived, Norman and his fellow-administrators were at last able to discard their uniforms, and become civilians.

When Herbert Samuel arrived, to take over from the Chief Administrator, General Sir Louis Bols, he was asked, by the General, to sign a receipt for the country. The copy of this receipt was sold, in recent years, to America. The statement — signed by Sir Louis, saying: 'Handed over to Sir Herbert Samuel, one Palestine, complete'—is in my possession.

The Arabs had placarded the country with notices declaring that Herbert Samuel would not be allowed to live for more than four days after his arrival.

On 8 June I wrote home:

If only Uncle Herbert would come immediately it would save a lot of mental and nervous strain. Everyone is longing for things to become settled and normal. It will be wonderful to have

167

someone in charge here in whom we can have complete confidence. Many of the officers never believed, till now, that England really meant to implement the Balfour Declaration, and some (among them a few of our greatest friends) have decided that they disagree so fundamentally with the policy that they are leaving. Unfortunately, some who also disagree are staying on, which won't make things easy.

There are to be three Secretaries, a Chief Secretary, a Financial Secretary and a Legal Secretary—Norman. Please send, as soon as possible, all the civilian clothes which he left at home. At last, he is to be out of khaki, and no longer 'Colonel', but plain 'Mister'. And we are to buy our own food—and to give up living on army rations.

Herbert Samuel arrived quite safely, on 30 June despite all the alarms and fears. On the day he arrived, armoured cars patrolled the town, aeroplanes skimmed over the house-tops, and police and soldiers were everywhere. The next day, we went to tea with him, privately, at Government House—the old OETA Headquarters on the Mount of Olives.

He was completely unperturbed, despite the threats of assassination. On the third day after his arrival we had planned another large reception following a legal conference, and had invited some four hundred guests. This time the reception was in the Municipal Gardens, on the Jaffa Road. And the High Commissioner (H.E. as he was now always called) declared his intention to be present. This rather staggered us: the gardens were in the middle of the town, surrounded by houses, many of them with flat roofs. The Jaffa Road was inadequately lit by a few lux lights. The police and secret service were terrifically busy all day, issuing countless 'confidential orders for safety' which, because Norman was busy with his conference, were all given to me. The whole road was closed to everyone, except those bringing their invitation cards. (I discovered later, to my regret, that the Mufti had been refused entrance as he had forgotten his card.) The military band struck up the National Anthem as H.E. arrived, with a motor-cycle escort, his ADC, and many policemen. Ronald Storrs and I took him round among the guests, whilst Norman selected those to be introduced among whom were some responsible for the threats against his life. He charmed them all by his friendliness and courtesy. I noticed that a bodyguard stood very near him all the time, with their hands on their revolvers. It was a most successful 'first appearance'—but both Norman and I suffered from nervous exhaustion when it was over.

The Arabs have great admiration for personal courage, and I believe his appearance on that evening, and his natural and friendly manner, had a genuine influence on their attitude towards him in the future. For five years he held the post of High Commissioner, and not once was there an attempt of his life.

It was a sad indication of the deterioration of feelings between Arabs and Jews that, in 1929, when Norman was shot and wounded by an Arab, the then High Commissioner, as well as the Government at home, decided that a Jewish Attorney-General was a liability, and that he could no longer remain in his post. He refused to resign, or to accept a Chief Justiceship elsewhere. After a miserable year in England, working at the Colonial Office, at the end of 1931 he was finally dismissed. He immediately accepted a professorship, on a part-time basis, at the Hebrew University in Jerusalem. It was then that our permanent home was in London, and my own life began to take a new turn.

HEADQUARTERS,
OCCUPIED ENEMY TERRITORY ADMINISTRATION (SOUTH),
JERUSALEM.

30. 6. 20.

Handed over to
Sir Herbert Samuel,
one Palestine, complete —

L. J. Bols.
Major General.

Statement signed by General Sir Louis Bols, Chief Administrator
of Palestine, and given to Sir Herbert Samuel